RAPID TEAM DEPLOYMENT

Building High-Performance Project Teams

Sandy Pokras

A FIFTY-MINUTE™ SERIES BOOK

CRISP PUBLICATIONS, INC.
Menlo Park, California

RAPID TEAM DEPLOYMENT
Building High-Performance Project Teams

Sandy Pokras

CREDITS
Managing Editor: **Kathleen Barcos**
Editor: **Kay Keppler**
Typesetting: **ExecuStaff**
Cover Design: **Carol Harris**
Artwork: **Ralph Mapson**

Copyright © 1995 by Viability Group Inc.

Printed in the United States of America by Bawden Printing Company.

English language Crisp books are distributed worldwide. Our major international distributors include:

CANADA: Reid Publishing Ltd., Box 69559—109 Thomas St., Oakville, Ontario, Canada L6J 7R4. TEL: (905) 842-4428, FAX: (905) 842-9327

Raincoast Books Distribution Ltd., 112 East 3rd Avenue, Vancouver, British Columbia, Canada V5T 1C8. TEL: (604) 873-6581, FAX: (604) 874-2711

AUSTRALIA: Career Builders, P.O. Box 1051, Springwood, Brisbane, Queensland, Australia 4127. TEL: 841-1061, FAX: 841-1580

NEW ZEALAND: Career Builders, P.O. Box 571, Manurewa, Auckland, New Zealand. TEL: 266-5276, FAX: 266-4152

JAPAN: Phoenix Associates Co., Mizuho Bldg. 2-12-2, Kami Osaki, Shinagawa-Ku, Tokyo 141, Japan. TEL: 3-443-7231, FAX: 3-443-7640

Selected Crisp titles are also available in other languages. Contact International Rights Manager Suzanne Kelly at (415) 323-6100 for more information.

Library of Congress Catalog Card Number 95-67039
Pokras, Sandy
Rapid Team Deployment
ISBN 1-56052-321-2

This book is printed on recyclable paper with soy ink.

ABOUT THIS BOOK

Rapid Team Deployment is not like most books. It has a unique "self-study" format that encourages a reader to become personally involved. Designed to be "read with a pencil," the book offers an abundance of exercises, activities, assessments and cases that invite participation.

This book presents a practical way to launch project teams and turn them into high-performance units that achieve quick success. Readers learn about team mechanics, proven principles, and group dynamics through results-oriented tools, how-tos and formulas for turning individuals into an effective team.

Rapid Team Deployment can be used effectively in a number of ways. Here are some possibilities:

► **Individual Study.** Because the book is self-instructional, all that is needed is a quiet place, some time and a pencil. By completing the activities and exercises, a reader should not only receive valuable feedback, but also take practical steps in creating a high performance work team.

► **Workshops and Seminars.** This book is ideal for reading prior to a workshop or seminar. With the basics in hand, the quality of participation will improve. More time can be spent in concept extensions and applications during the program. The book is also effective when a trainer distributes it at the beginning of a session and leads participants through the contents.

► **Remote Location Training.** Copies can be sent to those not able to attend "home office" training sessions.

There are other possibilities that depend on the objectives, program or ideas of the user. One thing is certain: even after it has been read, this book will serve as excellent reference material that can be easily reviewed.

Dedication—

This book is dedicated to the best team player I know, my wife Peg. Without her keeping our business and lives running while I was hacking away, I couldn't have written this book.

ABOUT THE AUTHOR

Sandy Pokras is president of Viability Group, Inc., a team building, communication training and management consulting firm in Northern California since 1973. His training workshops teach team managers, leaders, facilitators and members to achieve high-performance teamwork.

As a corporate consultant, program designer, keynote speaker, and conference facilitator, Mr. Pokras conducts sessions for a wide range of organizations, including IBM, Chevron, Federal Reserve Bank, Westinghouse, Siemens, University of California and the U.S. Postal Service.

Mr. Pokras is the author of numerous management articles as well as *Team Problem Solving,* published by Crisp Publications in 1991.

WELCOME TEAM BUILDERS!

Are you getting full value from your investment in teams? Probably not. Many organizations jump on the teamwork bandwagon only to fall off soon after hitting some rocks.

Do you find that:

- ✔ Team meetings take forever and get nowhere
- ✔ Resistance and conflict develop among the players
- ✔ Many of your teams bog down or self-destruct

Yet books, articles and conferences proclaim startling results from teams. You would be wise to ask, Are these stories for real?

The answer is a clear and solid yes! You can derive great benefits by applying high-performance team dynamics to projects and short-term assignments. But this process isn't instant, automatic or risk-free. Better questions to ask would be, Will the team approach work in my situation? If so, Will it be worth what I need to invest to make it work? If yes, then, How do I launch the team as quickly as possible yet insure it succeeds?

These questions explain the purpose of this book. In the following pages, you'll find answers that will help you deploy project teams for maximum impact.

Good teams are careful about defining roles. Since we want to practice what we preach, let's be clear about whom this book is intended for.

- Senior managers considering cross-functional team programs
- Mid-managers wanting to launch project teams and accelerate results
- Leaders who chair team meetings and manage projects
- Facilitators who guide the process and coach everyone involved

Whoever you are, if you work with teams, you'll benefit from what's presented here.

Sandy Pokras

CONTENTS

INTRODUCTION

Rapid Team Deployment focuses on teams with a definite lifecycle rather than self-directed natural work groups or management teams whose missions never end. This leaves a lot of territory. We'll talk about groups with short assignments as well as projects that take months or even years to complete. And we'll consider cross-functional teams as well as those wholly within your unit. Rapid team deployment (RTD) works with teams dedicated to:

- Implementation or discrete tasks

- Problem-solving or corrective action

- Statistical process control

- Business process reengineering

- New process development

- Quality or continuous improvement

- Employee involvement

- Benchmarking

- New product design and manufacture

- Concurrent engineering

You'll probably find other examples within your organization. Frankly, the names don't count. The mechanics we'll cover apply equally well, regardless of the mission of the team you want to improve. Although we won't discuss permanent teams, many of the tools that follow are necessary and vital to self-directed work teams.

Objectives Worksheet

To clarify your own expectations, please complete the following worksheet. Rate your objectives from 1 (low) to 10 (high).

PRIORITY   **OBJECTIVE**

_____ **1.** Decide when teamwork is appropriate and ensure it works within your organization's hierarchy.

_____ **2.** Organize, launch and lead project teams to achieve their performance objectives.

_____ **3.** Use the right tools to follow the team lifecycle.

_____ **4.** Employ the critical success factors of high-performance teams and avoid the worst pitfalls.

_____ **5.** Accelerate team progress to achieve results as quickly as possible.

_____ **6.** Monitor and measure performance to keep the team on track and maintain accountability.

_____ **7.** Deploy results when ready and disband the team.

Asking you to prioritize objectives should emphasize that this is really a workbook. We won't spend lots of time on theory. Instead, our limited space will focus on practical applications. In fact, you'll soon select a case study from your own situation, so be prepared. We will also trace the story of an organization in a position that may not be too different from yours.

P A R T

I

Defining Team Direction

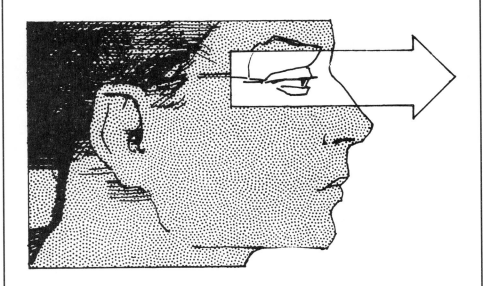

TEAM MECHANICS

Before we run off to "do teams," let's clarify what we mean. Many people think of a team as a task force, which is a temporary grouping of individuals asked to assist an accountable person in carrying out a specific assignment. When you need cross-functional expertise, a task force can work. But if only one person is accountable, we're not talking true teamwork and trend-setting accomplishments.

For others, a team is a committee, a continuing meeting of parties chosen to consider a specific subject and make recommendations, but typically without authority to act. A committee's updates, information transfers and exploratory discussions can be valuable, but teamwork implies ownership and commitment.

Team Definition

Here's the definition of a team we're striving to achieve. A team is a group of willing and trained individuals who are:

- United around a common goal

- Depending on each other to achieve it

- Structured to work together

- Sharing responsibility for their task

- Empowered to implement decisions

Team members can't be ordered; they must be willing. A team's unity stems from the challenging goal the members accept. They share responsibility, authority and accountability because they can't get their job done alone. They decide by consensus, which means everyone agrees and no one loses when they differ. They have power to implement decisions, because without it, they probably won't do a very good job.

MEET THE ABC GROUP

The ABC Group is an organization whose mission is to eliminate international cultural barriers through language instruction. Their research proved that people who can recognize and use 400 words of a foreign language not only cope in another country, but make friends easily. Modern microchip and speech recognition technology have opened doors for cross-cultural communication, but they also present hard choices for ABC's leadership.

The ABC Group has operated as a not-for-profit think tank. Now that its initial grant funding has lapsed, the company's leaders want to capitalize on the profit potential they see. Unfortunately, many employees would rather operate the old way—which didn't emphasize rapid results.

The need for change is urgent, and RTD is top management's strategy. The good news for team players is that ABC already launched several empowered teams to help plan its future. The bad news is that some are floundering. It will require some serious team-building to sort out this mess.

Throughout this book, we will follow teams from ABC Group through the RTD cycle.

CASE STUDY: ABC's Teams

ABC Group started off two of its teams—the strategic planning team and the marketing team—on the right foot. Terry, the CEO, asked for volunteers for each team from select departments. In their first meeting, the strategic planning team divided their big assignment into smaller tasks that qualified members could handle. In a follow-up meeting the next day, Terry approved their initial proposals, asking them to devote 35% of their time to the strategic planning team.

The marketing team consisted of one volunteer each from the marketing, finance, computer, manufacturing and quality control departments. At their first meeting, Chris, the new marketing director, seemed preoccupied. Although the members were initially excited about their general goal, enthusiasm waned when Chris couldn't explain what they were supposed to do. Only two of the team members knew anything about marketing and couldn't understand their role. In response to questions, Chris directed everyone to talk to their immediate supervisors, who knew even less about the marketing team.

Which parts of the definition of a team apply to these two ABC teams?

_____

_____

EXERCISE: *High-Performance Teamwork*

Think about the teams you've been involved with. Did any of them operate well? This book will show you how to build the 13 following characteristics of a high-performance unit. Use this list to plan team-building, measure a team's performance level or decide how much time you have for team development. Measure performance on a scale of 1 to 10, with 1 being poor, 5 being average, and 10 being excellent.

#	CHARACTERISTIC	DESCRIPTION	RATING
1.	Purpose	A clear, challenging and inspiring common purpose	_____
2.	Membership	Complete, willing, skilled, available and trained membership	_____
3.	Leadership	Principled leadership with high standards to build the team and guide results until the team takes charge	_____
4.	Structure	A flexible, defined, results-oriented structure of roles, processes and procedures under team control	_____
5.	Plans	Long- and short-range plans based on a team road-map with measurable milestones	_____
6.	Participation	Active participation of all team members who follow through	_____
7.	Communication	Open communication and informed members	_____
8.	Trust	Mutual trust, support and collaboration so that teammates support each other	_____
9.	Consensus	Critical decisions by consensus, especially when differences produce conflict	_____
10.	Ownership	Joint ownership, entrepreneurial spirit and shared responsibility for implementation	_____
11.	Synergy	Active cooperation between team members	_____
12.	Recognition	Appropriate rewards, frequent recognition and routine celebrations	_____
13.	Empowerment	Sufficient empowerment to enable the team to achieve its mission	_____

STAGES OF TEAM DEVELOPMENT

High performance, or any team performance at all, is not instant nor automatic. Groups have development stages.

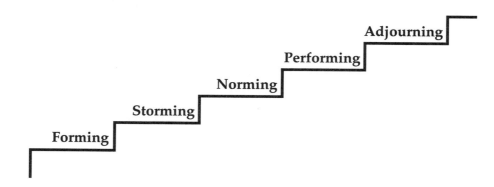

No matter how skilled you are at launching teams or how experienced their members are, forming groups tend to act shy, tentative and uncertain. They might even be anxious and suspicious. There's not a lot of energy, investment or work accomplished very quickly. This forming stage is often frustrating for task-oriented managers who want instant results and don't know how to accelerate this process. This is where ABC's teams, like all others, started off.

If you succeed at building interest and commitment to work together, your reward is storming. Storming teams are much more open, but not usually very positive. They tend to complain, criticize and disagree. The good news is that they're getting involved and communicating, although it's not yet the kind of team spirit you'd hoped for. Team-builders who don't know how to facilitate storming can decide that teams are ineffective and disband them before they have a chance to accomplish anything.

Norming teams shift their attention from internal tensions to their work challenge. As they resolve their differences, relationships improve. They can express themselves positively even when they have problems. Norming teams don't have all the answers, but they make steady progress in learning how to tackle their job. At last, you're probably thinking, this is what you wanted in the first place.

Performing teams rate high on all 13 characteristics of the Team Performance Rating Form (page 13). These people aren't just getting the job done, they're totally committed, coordinated and cooperative. They are a self-regulating, self-sufficient and self-directed unit, and nothing can stop them from achieving their purpose. Obviously, it takes time and work to arrive here. The more skilled the team-building approach, the more rapid the team's ultimate deployment.

When your high-performance team accomplishes its purpose, you'll face another problem: adjourning. Performing teams don't want to break up, and maybe they shouldn't. You've got to do something with all this excitement and ability—either recharter this group or use the team members as the nucleus of new projects. Otherwise you'll have trouble recruiting teams in the future.

Team Performance Accelerators

You can't create a high-performance team by edict. It takes action and effort. We will explore three sets of proven tools for team development: defining roles, planning the team's work and maximizing participation. The following chart introduces the tools and structures that accelerate team operations.

ROLE DEFINITION	
Leaders	*Team Sponsor* The manager who owns the team's territory and champions its work
	Team Facilitator Group process expert assigned to coach, train and guide the team
	Team Leader Elected or appointed team member who builds the team
Members	*Team Members* Active owners who collect data, decide jointly, assign action and report
	Meeting Hats Rotating assignments that keep meetings functioning efficiently
	Work Functions Skill specialties inherited or developed to implement team decisions

STAGES OF TEAM DEVELOPMENT
(continued)

PLANNING TOOLS	
Charter	Statement of the team's mission, challenge and mechanics serving as common goal and contract
Roadmap	Measurable objectives defining what the team will deliver according to a master plan
Public Relations	Targets and actions to insure that customers, suppliers and stakeholders work with the team

PARTICIPATION TOOLS	
Meeting Tools	Agendas, discussion moderation and process reviews
Ground Rules	Values established by a team to guide behavior
Brainstorming	Quick, creative idea generation without judgment or evaluation
Data Analysis	Input, research, data collection and experiments so that decisions are made by fact
Consensus	Joint decisions that merge opinions, resolve conflict, satisfy all needs and are supported

Which of these components did ABC's teams start with? Terry probably will play the sponsor's role and volunteers will be team members. But do any of them know their function? As for planning, maybe the strategic planning team did a bit and was at least aware of public relations by calling a swift follow-up meeting with Terry. They probably used some participation tools to be able to arrive at some decisions so quickly. Though willing, there's little evidence that the marketing team knew much about high performance.

TO TEAM OR NOT TO TEAM?

Before you launch a team, decide why you're doing it and why it's a good idea. When a team's purpose is clear, you can plan and organize the effort so that minimum time and effort are wasted. You'll be able to brief the team better so it can hit the ground running.

Team Goals

There are seven reasons you might want to launch a team.

► **RESULTS**

Increasing output and productivity or improving service and quality

► **EFFICIENCY**

Lowering costs, reducing cycle time, eliminating waste and solving problems

► **SYNERGY**

Combining brainpower and increasing creativity by getting different disciplines to work together

► **WORKING RELATIONSHIPS**

Improving communication, cooperation and consensus

► **ATTITUDES**

Improving morale, job satisfaction and the willingness to raise performance standards

► **EMPOWERMENT**

Involving workers in decisions, increasing span of control and raising everyone's sense of responsibility

► **CROSS-FUNCTIONAL WORK**

Confronting cross-departmental issues and multidisciplinary problems using outside resources and expertise

ABC's strategic planning team was set up for the first reason, fast strategic planning results. Its marketing team, on the other hand, could be focused on any of the other goals. The lesson is clear: Figure out what you want the team to achieve. If you don't know why you're forming a team, don't expect quick success.

TO TEAM OR NOT TO TEAM? (continued)

Team Costs

You have decided you want to accomplish one or more of the above goals. Before continuing with RTD, consider alternatives. You could:

- Do the work yourself

- Ignore the issue and hope it goes away

- Delegate to a qualified individual

- Form a task force under an accountable person's control

- Escalate to higher management

- Hire a consultant

- Charter a high-performance team

A high-performance team offers the best long-term benefits, but it takes work and time (weeks or months) to build a team to top performance. To decide how much team building you'll invest in, first consider the resources, support and obstacle resolution needed. When you launch a team, you're really committing to provide:

- ▶ **Labor.** Part of teamwork is work away from production, also requiring skilled team leadership, expert technical support and team facilitation

- ▶ **Time Investment.** Team members need time for meetings, data collection, outside preparations, coaching sessions and documentation

- ▶ **Lead Time.** Teams need time for members to move up their learning curves and the overall team to learn to work together before they get results

- ▶ **Management Input.** The team's manager needs to brief, train, guide, monitor and stay in touch to keep the team informed

- ▶ **Management Support.** Management needs to give up some direct control and concentrate on providing rewards and recognition

- ▶ **Relationships.** Teams need training as a group, opportunities for face-to-face communication and conflict resolution skills

- ▶ **Obstacle Resolution.** Expect to meet resistance to change, reluctance to share information, distrust, insecurity and unwillingness to take risks

With management approval, ABC's strategic planning team allocated 35% of its time to team activities. Terry offered to be available when they needed input or support. Strategic planning team members started off feeling that there was a future in being on the team, and that Terry wouldn't let it fail. What do you think the marketing team was saying about how much Chris wanted to invest in it?

Cost/Benefit Analysis

Is the cost worth the potential benefit of starting a team? Ask yourself if you have time for the necessary meetings, training, planning, supporting, coaching and troubleshooting. If you can invest in team-building now, plan big and hope for huge rewards later. If you need quick results with untrained people, scale back your expectations. Too many managers announce that they're forming a high-performance, totally empowered team before they consider costs. After starting the process, they back out. As a result, many teams start at a crawl and then slow down because of insufficient resources.

EMPOWERMENT

Good ABC news! Terry just talked with Chris about the value of teamwork in the new marketing department. Chris's cost-benefit analysis concluded that teaming will be worth it. Like Chris's, your biggest risk probably will be the trust you have to place in, and the control you have to give up to, the team. Teamwork is all about getting involved in something worthwhile that members feel they can influence. Traditionally, managers like Chris decide and direct while commanding and controlling their territory. Operate that way without giving any power to the team and you'll see slow death, not rapid deployment, and teamwork.

What Is Empowerment?

To empower means to give official authority, delegate legal power or give faculties or abilities to enable. In this illustration, just outside the bull's-eye, the second ring is the target of empowered teamwork. The ring of barriers shows what's in the way.

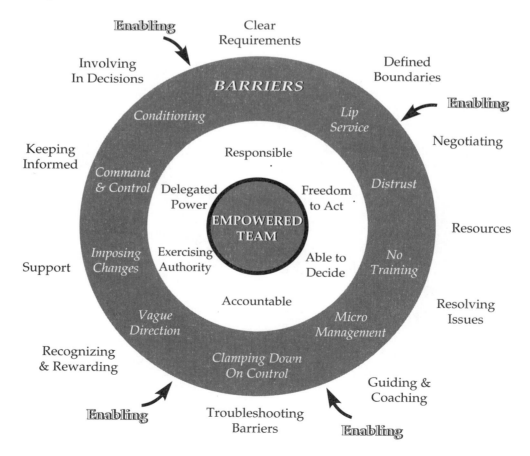

How To Empower and Enable

Empowerment isn't absolute. Teamwork means sharing power. Your job is to define what the team will be responsible for, what their authority will be and what management's role will be. The cost of empowerment is clearly communicating goals, requirements and boundaries from the start.

Empowering a team is challenging, and doing RTD is more so. Employees are conditioned to receiving direction. How can you direct them to be productive without outside direction? How can you enable them to accomplish things that others haven't?

Empowerment really means:

- Giving workers authority, influence and control over their own destiny

- Involving people in decisions that affect them

- Creating ownership and commitment to their team charter

- Allowing them the freedom to implement their own decisions

- Making them responsible and holding them accountable

- Helping them find their own way out of conflict instead of clamping down

Lip service alone won't do much to empower a team. Teams must be enabled to achieve their mission by your:

- Giving clear general direction without being overly prescriptive

- Negotiating instead of imposing a team charter

- Providing training and support to develop potential

- Giving time, tools, money, space and equipment

- Helping them consider new options when they make hard choices

- Removing barriers and troubleshooting problems they can't control

- Rewarding initiative, innovation, cooperation and risk taking

PLANNING EMPOWERMENT LEVEL

A valuable team-launching exercise is to plan what you want them involved in before they start. Use the Team Empowerment Worksheet to plan what teams should work on now and what you hope they get to in the future. (Note the blank lines at the bottom for activities peculiar to a specific team.)

Team Empowerment Worksheet

#	TEAM ACTIVITY	NOW	FUTURE
1.	Membership selection		
2.	Team charter development		
3.	Team project plan		
4.	Team budget		
5.	Training plans		
6.	Meeting schedule		
7.	Meeting agendas		
8.	Meeting evaluation		
9.	Problem analysis		
10.	Solution decision		
11.	Selling team proposals		
12.	Implementation control		
13.	Procedure documentation		
14.	Performance review		
15.	Team rewards		
16.	Measurement of results		
17.	Communication		
18.			
19.			
20.			

CASE STUDY: ABC Team Update

Do you agree that Terry empowered the strategic planning team from the start? When put to the test, Terry supported the team by approving its first proposals.

Terry urged Chris to work through the team process. Chris admitted to moving slowly on empowering the marketing team. Chris was concerned about turning the design of ABC's new marketing system over to a group of novices, but after talking to Terry, Chris decided to narrow the marketing team's focus to researching markets and distribution methods for their potential products. This arena was ideal for the team, since this type of marketing needed lots of work that Chris couldn't do while setting up the department.

In a second team meeting, Chris apologized for the vague start and suggested the research role for the team. Several members finally understood why they were there. Terry explained the work that management still needed to do to clarify direction. Chris committed to attending all meetings and guiding the marketing team's efforts.

In response, most of the team remarked that they felt much better about knowing how to contribute, but one member challenged the new deal by asking, "If you believe in teamwork, why can't you trust us to get the job done without attending all team meetings?" Chris pointed out that management input and marketing expertise was vital in the beginning and that things could change later. Chris asked the team what they thought. The consensus was clear that they wanted Chris there until further notice.

EXERCISE AHEAD

EXERCISE: *Case Study Team Selection*

It's time for you to choose a real situation to use throughout this book to apply the tools and principles presented.

1. Review the reasons teams are formed (Team Goals from page 9) and then decide which are needed in your organization. List these goals on the left side of the Cost/Benefit Analysis Worksheet.

2. Calculate what you'll have to invest to achieve these goals using teamwork (Team Costs from page 10) and list them on the right side of the worksheet.

3. Consider which situations seem like a good investment. Which do you believe warrant team-building? Which would serve as a good learning example as well?

4. Select one example to serve as your Case Study Team. Decide firmly, since we'll delve into this case study. Record your choice at the bottom of the worksheet.

Cost/Benefit Analysis Worksheet

Benefits of Teamwork Desired	Costs of Deploying This Team

Case Study Team

RAPID TEAM DEPLOYMENT

Few three-month project teams ever reach high performance and total self-sufficiency. Members can't spend six weeks getting ready. Neither do you want them to storm for weeks, throw away most of their resources and then slap together a last-minute proposal that no one wants to implement anyway. That's not the idea of RTD, but their project can still benefit from cooperation, collaboration and synergy.

You might have the best intentions in the world when you announce you're forming an empowered self-directed team. But consider:

- ✔ Do you want the team to rework the basic processes you use to produce your product or service?

- ✔ Will the team be ready right away to work directly with your customers?

- ✔ Do you want the team to dictate what to say to your senior management?

- ✔ Will you give them full budget control?

- ✔ If you can't answer "yes" right now, when will you be able to?

If you have any hesitation in answering these questions, don't make claims you won't substantiate. Don't call the team empowered, because they'll think that's absolute. Don't tell them they're self-directed if you ever intend to redirect their efforts when you or your boss become dissatisfied. Don't tell them to do what they think is best if you ever might respond, "That's not what I wanted you to do."

Our Theme

The theme of RTD is simple: Build and empower the team to the degree possible for the time you're willing to invest in team development. Define the task and its boundaries, organize the team accordingly and give them only essential tools. RTD is all about getting a group to rise to the occasion by concentrating narrowly.

Realize there's a business equation at work. Make your calculations wisely and stay the course. Decide which team-building tools will help you achieve your purpose. Be realistic about natural growth cycles, and don't initiate a team unless the situation warrants the investment. If it doesn't, find another means to get the job done.

RAPID TEAM DEPLOYMENT (continued)

Two Examples

Example #1: You're launching a two-year project team to introduce a new service, you've got time for natural team growth. You'll want to invest in all the high-performance components you can to help you get the most out of this vital team. Let them spend more time on planning. Send them off to week-long retreats to work on it. Give them access to lots of experts. Encourage them to use experimental personality-style surveys and attend wilderness survival experiences. Feed them all sorts of information and regular updates. Be patient with their internal struggles. You can make the case that team-building will pay in the long run.

Example #2: You've got a three-month project and must choose the tools that fit that situation. Give your team more specific directions, established checkpoints and defined resources. Make their initial training more focused. Watch them closely and keep reminding them of their challenge, but don't distract them with irrelevant information or micromanagement. With the right support, expect that they'll build to an adequate level of performance. They don't have the time to grow into a world-class model in a few weeks, so don't encourage them to spend much time on longer-term concerns. Help them confront their urgent task now.

How To Do It

To deploy a project team as quickly as possible with the highest chance of success and maximum synergy, you—the team's manager—need a game plan. What exactly do you want the team to accomplish? Who needs to be involved? How much empowerment do you want to give them? What information do they need and how will you get it to them? How much time can you all invest in developing teamwork? How will you stay in touch without smothering them? What will you do to support them and run interference?

Then you need to give them the right amount of time, information and resources for their project. Guide them to plan, define roles, and build participation at the right depth for their task. RTD will give you the entire formula for building the highest performance level possible.

THE TEAM ENVIRONMENT

If everyone in your organization was skilled and experienced at sponsoring, leading, facilitating and participating in high-performance teams, teams could be deployed much faster. The military uses this rapid-deployment-force model to prepare for all contingencies. To build a universal team environment:

► Train all management levels, functional groups and employee disciplines in high-performance teamwork

► Launch narrowly focused demonstration projects that let newcomers learn and practice

► Staff a team support unit to plan and conduct training, troubleshoot problems and make available proven team processes

► Maintain an up-to-date database of training, assignments and experience

► Rotate everyone into different team roles to build depth

► Regulate team commitments so that a pool of qualified team members is always available for rapid deployment and no one is overcommitted

Though these efforts are most conducive to long-term team efforts, they may not be the ideal place for you to start using RTD.

DEFINING TEAM REQUIREMENTS

Team Lifecycle

By making it this far, you've decided teamwork is warranted for your project and will be worth the investment. Now your challenge will be to guide the new team through the Team Lifecycle.

This flowchart says that you first must give the project a clear sense of direction, get the group recruited and organized, invest some time and effort in team-building to fuse individuals into a cohesive unit and then let them demonstrate effective teamwork that won't be perfect so you'll use continuous improvement until they have to wrap up. This description defines the agenda we'll follow to present RTD.

Team Direction

Before you can form a team, you'll need to brief potential members on the organization's critical business need, its overall strategy and where their goals fit in. Without clear objectives, it is nearly impossible to recruit skilled and committed members.

Too wide a scope is another common mistake that slows teams down. Yet most of us tend to dump all sorts of elaborate demands on an as-yet-untested group and then get angry when it flounders. We should know better, and yet it happens over and over. Err on the side of narrow requirements. Give a new team a chance for small wins before you expect it to conquer the world.

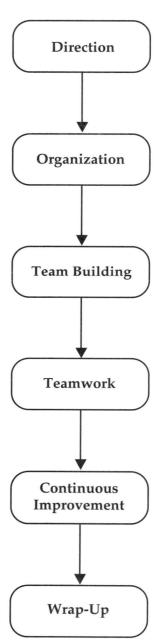

REQUIREMENTS TECHNIQUES

Let's review three techniques for defining team requirements.

Technique		Definition
#1: Mission Statement	➡	The team's purpose
#2: Customer Requirements	➡	What the customer expects
#3: Team Deliverables	➡	Measurable end products

Why remind you of things you're probably already aware of? Because you need to use one or all of these methods to clarify what you want the team to be account-able for. Teamwork requires clear goal-setting, since the message must be com-municated to different people from diverse backgrounds. Your aim is to unify the new group around these requirements once communicated.

Here's the rub: Define the requirements too thoroughly and you disempower the team. Define the requirements too vaguely and the team flounders. You're looking for the right balance. Draft your best requirement statements and be prepared to negotiate once team members form their own opinions.

For example, let's say Chris tells ABC's marketing team to study only high-tech catalog sales and work exclusively through an old friend's distribution company. Wouldn't you question the value of this team? But "improving marketing" is much too vague a direction for ABC's conflicted position. Let's see how the three requirements techniques can help Chris.

REQUIREMENTS TECHNIQUES (continued)

Requirements Technique #1: Mission Statement

A mission statement should briefly define the team's customer and the customer's need, what product or service the team must deliver to meet the need and how the team should deliver that product or service.

Here is the mission that ABC's strategic planning team developed:

To develop a business plan that everyone with a stake in ABC's future supports.

The marketing team initially tried the following mission statement:

To explore marketing options for ABC.

They found that was far too broad. The team narrowed it to:

Establish a distribution system to meet the needs of internal departments that will get ABC's future products into the hands of external customers as quickly and economically as possible.

This worksheet can help you construct your own mission statement.

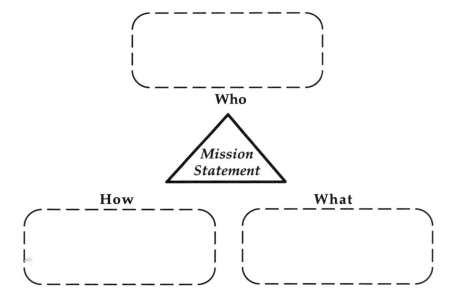

Organizational missions typically aren't measurable. Instead, a mission statement defines why the team is formed, what it exists for and where it should head. By suggesting a general mission statement, you can define direction now and remain open enough to negotiate exact accountability later.

Requirements Technique #2: Customer Requirements

Another way to define the team's requirements is by using the customer-supplier chain as this diagram shows . . .

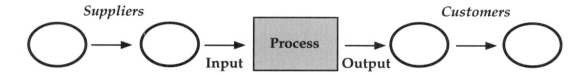

Here's what these symbols stand for.

► **Input**   What you need to get your job done

► **Supplier**   People, functions and departments (internal and external) from whom you receive inputs

► **Process**   The sequence actions that constitute your job function

► **Output**   The products that you create

► **Customers** People, functions and departments (internal and external) who consume (receive, utilize, value and benefit from) your outputs

REQUIREMENTS TECHNIQUES (continued)

Use the Customer Requirement Worksheet as a guide to this technique. If you start by determining what outputs or services you expect from the team, you can discover who consumes those outputs. By asking these internal or external customers how they will judge successful results, you can define specific requirements for the team. Typically these take the form of satisfaction factors like volume, quality, cycle time, prompt delivery or other specifications.

Customer Requirement Worksheet

OUTPUTS	CUSTOMERS	REQUIREMENTS

The strategic planning team's mission statement already specifies an output, a business plan. They used this worksheet to define categories of customers and what they each would like to see in a business plan. Top management wanted a short executive summary with conclusions supported by data and analysis. The engineers wanted everything presented in flowcharts. Manufacturing employees wanted simple statements of how their operations would change. From these deliberations, the team planned the best format for the document.

Requirements Technique #3: Team Deliverables

"Deliverable" means a measurable product or output that is completed and turned over to the customer.

Use these questions to define team deliverables.

1. What output does the team need to deliver?

2. What outcome is expected from the project?

3. What final product will be valuable to the customer?

4. What are the customer's requirements?

5. How will the customer decide acceptability?

6. What major milestones must be met?

7. What long-, medium- and short-term objectives are established?

8. What are the project's deadlines?

9. How will the team sponsor measure success?

10. What continuing product or service is desired?

Even if mission statements and customer requirements aren't measurable enough for short-term accountability, deliverables must be. Deliverables are best defined as SMART objectives:

Specific

Measurable

Agreed-upon

Result-oriented

Timed

REQUIREMENTS TECHNIQUES (continued)

Record your answers to the 10 questions on page 25 on the SMART Worksheet to complete this method of defining requirements.

SMART Worksheet

Accomplishment: *What do you want the team to achieve?*
Specific: What do you want them to accomplish?
Measurable: How will you monitor progress?
Agreed-Upon: How will this deliverable satisfy each team member's needs?
Result: What is the finished product or final outcome?
Time-Bound: How long will it take to complete?
DELIVERABLE: Rewrite the deliverable to include all the above.

CASE STUDY: ABC's SMARTs

Here's how ABC's marketing team used the worksheet . . .

SMART Worksheet for ABC's Marketing Team

Accomplishment: What do you want the team to achieve?

A product distribution system

Specific: What do you want them to accomplish?

U.S. and European distributor agreements that move products to customers

Measurable: How will you monitor progress?

Routinely calculate and graph the number and value of products shipped

Agreed-Upon: How will this deliverable satisfy each team member's needs?

Both number and value of ABC's three products are needed to satisfy engineering, manufacturing, marketing and finance

Result: What is the finished product or final outcome?

Increasing shipments of the three key products will prove that distribution channels are working

Time-Bound: How long will it take to complete?

Six months

DELIVERABLE: Rewrite the deliverable to include all the above.

Within six months, ABC's marketing team will be able to show increasing shipments of its three key products to U.S. and European distributors based on graphs of number and value of units shipped

EXERCISE: *Team Requirements*

Let's use these direction-setting tools to define requirements for your case study team.

1. Decide if one, two or all three of the techniques presented will best guide you in forming and recruiting the team.

2. Work through the worksheets you choose.

3. Rewrite the results below.

Your Case Study Team Requirements Worksheet

_____

_____

_____

_____

_____

_____

_____

MANAGEMENT SUPPORT ROLES

If you've been able to work through the case study exercises so far, then you're probably the team's sponsor. A team sponsor is typically the manager who:

- Is responsible for the team's problem or process

- Is primarily responsible to a customer for a product or service

- Controls the territory's resources by role or by delegation

- Chooses to seek solutions or improvements through teamwork

- Has the authority to approve or reject team recommendations

- Champions the team

Team Sponsor Functions

An effective team sponsor initiates and supports a team by:

- Providing direction and guidance

- Negotiating the team charter

- Authorizing time and resources

- Coaching the team leader

- Staying in touch and monitoring progress

- Holding the team accountable

- Committing to follow through and promote team success

- Supporting whatever the team decides to implement

- Clearing roadblocks and removing barriers

- Recognizing and rewarding team accomplishments

MANAGEMENT SUPPORT ROLES (continued)

To do this, a team sponsor has seven distinct functions.

1. DIRECTION

Clarify higher management goals and organization needs, brief the team, present requirements and boundaries and define authority and empowerment levels

2. ENABLING

Provide adequate tools, training and resources; authorize ample team-member work time; permit team development; allow the team decision-making authority and don't impose unrealistic time constraints

3. SUPPORT

Honor team needs and desires by being open to changes and being willing to negotiate and take risks the team thinks are necessary, and by expecting to approve and implement what the team proposes

4. GUIDANCE

Monitor team progress and problems; encourage small, quick wins to build confidence; advise, coach and support instead of demanding and directing and keep the team informed

5. FOLLOW-THROUGH

Read team minutes, meet with team leaders, occasionally attend team meetings, respond to team questions, receive presentations positively, be consistent with commitments

6. REMOVE BARRIERS

Accept setbacks without overreacting; run interference, remove obstacles and clear roadblocks; let the team handle problems when appropriate

7. CHAMPION THE TEAM

Serve as the team's management liaison, advocate team solutions, reward and acknowledge team efforts and participate in team celebrations

If this looks like a lot of work, it is. Eventually a high-performance team will relieve you of much of this work, but it doesn't happen instantly or automatically. You're committing to do these seven sponsor functions in return for the team committing to achieve their charter. That takes work from everyone.

TASK VS. TEAM FOCUS

One of the many choices a team sponsor has to make is whether to emphasize task results or team building.

Ideally, you want both, but by starting any team-building at all, you're accepting the challenge of balancing time for project work against team development. When the balance is off, these consequences might occur.

Examples of too much TASK focus	Possible Consequences
• Total focus on work and task by the project manager • Pushing the team for results members are not ready to produce • Too much pressure on deadlines and efficiency	• Some team members remain uncomfortable • Conflicts are ignored and creativity suffers • Dominators run meetings with little participation from others
Examples of too much TEAM focus	**Possible Consequences**
• Personal problems absorb a lot of team meeting time • Team meetings become nonstop gripe sessions • Frequent blocked consensus stalls team progress	• The team makes very little progress on its project • Action items never get done without repercussions • Deadlines are ignored and checkpoints are missed

TOP 10 SPONSOR GUIDELINES

TOP 10 TEAM SPONSOR GUIDELINES

1. Charter teams you intend to support and no others. When you empower a team, consider that providing adequate information, resources, training, time, guidance and support are a moral obligation.

2. Clarify your expectations, boundaries and performance standards when you start. Guide, update and reinforce teams so you never have to say no.

3. Be assertive about what you need and want from teams, but be willing to negotiate about how they want to proceed.

4. Keep teams informed and let them know how they're doing, but don't micromanage.

5. Attend occasional team meetings when invited or for scheduled agenda items, honoring their ground rules and meeting mechanics. Avoid vague or conflicting feedback to individual team members about public team business.

6. Hold teams accountable but recognize their achievements too. Uphold agreements with teams and don't change priorities midstream unless unexpected developments warrant it.

7. Build mutual trust by treating team members as equals and avoiding intimidation tactics. Encourage openness about problems by coaching, not punishing.

8. Don't make unilateral decisions when teams can decide. Avoid knee-jerk reactions when teams may be able to self-correct on their own.

9. Whenever possible, say yes and take swift action on team proposals, or advise on adjustments needed to win approval.

10. Report team progress and proposals to upper management with pride, giving them full credit, total support and deserved recognition.

UPPER MANAGEMENT'S IMPACT ON TEAMWORK

Even if you sign-up wholeheartedly for the demanding job of team sponsor, your team may still run into management support problems that slow teamwork immeasurably. What if:

- Cross-functional bosses won't let their members attend meetings?

- Other units won't cooperate because of other priorities?

- Your team's work adds to others' stress?

- Needed resources are under the control of uninvolved people?

It's easy to say that your job, team sponsor, is to champion the team and remove barriers. But what if upper management disagrees?

Steering Council Function

Teams deploy more rapidly and thrive more fully when overseen by a strong team steering council. A steering council is a model management team composed of team sponsors or their bosses who are responsible for planning and guiding how their organization implements, applies and integrates teamwork.

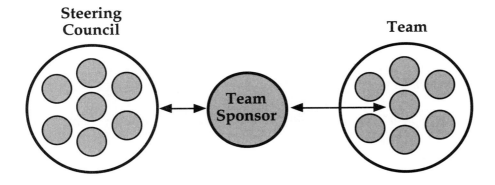

This diagram shows the team sponsor as the communication link between the steering council and the team. Whether team sponsors are members of the council or report directly to council members, they must represent consensus from above while guiding the team.

UPPER MANAGEMENT'S IMPACT ON TEAMWORK (continued)

Ideal World

Ideally, a team steering council would:

- Establish vision, strategy and long-range plans

- Prioritize business issues that teams should address

- Authorize resources and coordinate training

- Oversee the chartering of teams by their members

- Develop and continuously improve the teamwork process

- Monitor team progress and troubleshoot problems

- Support team efforts and drive cross-functional cooperation

- Publicize results and deploy lessons learned

- Provide recognition and rewards.

If all your peers deploy high-performance teams, everyone's customers and suppliers will understand and cooperate. Your bosses will back you up. Your marketing department will extol your praises. Your end users will crave your improved quality.

What if you don't live in an ideal world? Without a steering council, it seems you've committed to taking on some of their functions on your own. You need to enlist your boss, his or her peers and upper management to support your team.

Although this sounds like a daunting task at first, think about what you'll do if your team hits a political wall midway through the project. Smoothing the path for the team may, in the long run, turn out to be relatively cost-effective insurance.

CASE STUDY: ABC Update

Your immediate opinion might be that ABC's strategic management team wouldn't have a steering council. However, ABC's board of directors and all department heads should strongly influence what a strategic planning team does. As for the marketing team, because their requirements affect several key departments, they will need support from nearly every director.

Terry and Chris decided to convene another team, which they called the ABC Team Steering Council, composed of board representatives and all departments heads. In this way, these two initial project teams, and all future ones, will have a management support structure to help clarify direction, back team sponsors and set priorities as the teams get underway.

EXERCISE: Management Support Roles

Let's apply what we've covered to your Case Study Team.

1. Who is the best choice for Case Study Team sponsor? You? Someone above or below you in the hierarchy?

   _____

2. Why? List the qualifications of your recommended team sponsor from the role definition and functions on page 32 to back up your choice.

   _____

   _____

3. Which management team already fulfills the functions as your Case Study Team's steering council?

   _____

4. If none, list the managers whose understanding, involvement and support are needed for the Case Study Team to succeed.

   _____

   _____

5. How will you secure support from these managers and protect the team to insure it can flourish in as positive an environment as possible?

   _____

   _____

ESTABLISHING TEAM LEADERSHIP

Leading is different from managing. Leading means to show the way by going first and to guide direction by persuasion. Managing implies command and control. Leaders concentrate on getting others to learn, grow and win. Managers concentrate on getting results because their bosses expect it. We all know there's a time for both leading and managing, but the stark truth is that leading a team effectively in the short run produces both growth and results in the long run. Command and control may get immediate results, but unfortunately only the manager, not the team, is motivated for the next assignment.

So when we talk about a team leader, we mean an elected or appointed team member who builds the team and guides joint action on its work. Note we're not talking about an authority figure or a supervisor, but a team member who has a unique function. Some of the characteristics frequently reported of good leaders are:

✔ **Visionary**	✔ **Dependable**
✔ **Dedicated**	✔ **Objective**
✔ **Communicative**	✔ **Positive**
✔ **Good Listener**	✔ **Open**
✔ **Coach**	✔ **Involving**
✔ **Role Model**	✔ **Initiator**

At ABC, a heated discussion broke out when Chris claimed he would function as both marketing team sponsor and team leader. Several other directors claimed that the team would never grow if Chris, with superior marketing expertise and all the power, wore too many hats. Chris objected that they wouldn't know what to do without knowledge and guidance. The decision was tabled until after more training.

Team Leader Functions

A team leader initially inherits five functions when accepting the role.

► **TEAM BUILDER**

Assess team health, plan training, unify the group, build team spirit and mutual trust, resolve conflicts and adjust membership if necessary

► **TEAM MEMBERS' COACH**

Meet individually with all members, motivate, reinforce positive behavior, give advice and orient new members

► **WORK COORDINATOR**

Clarify sponsor goals, help complete plans, insure roles are filled, guide data collection, keep team on track and troubleshoot problems

► **MEETING CHAIR**

Plan, organize and chair meetings; ensure public recording of ideas; facilitate team consensus; assign action items and distribute minutes

► **PUBLIC RELATIONS ORGANIZER**

Identify stakeholders, assign team representatives, plan reporting, coordinate contacts, solicit input and feedback and conduct presentations

Since good team leaders are dedicated to working themselves out of a job, their attention is always on delegating. The sooner that team members can take over these tasks, the higher the performance level of the team. In a truly world-class team, the team leader is merely a figurehead, since leadership is distributed, shared and rotated to whomever is best qualified for a specific function.

ESTABLISHING TEAM LEADERSHIP (continued)

Team Leader Selection

A team sponsor can appoint whomever they think would serve as the best team leader or let the team choose. Both methods have advantages.

METHOD	ADVANTAGES	DISADVANTAGES
Appointed	• Management support is more likely • Forming teams get more immediate direction • Team can make faster progress if skilled leader is chosen	• Team may not follow leader • Chemistry may be wrong • Appointment of wrong person can backfire
Elected	• Team members know their needs • Natural leaders may appear • Team member support more likely • Encourages empowerment	• Takes time • May cause competition • Choice may be for the wrong reasons

The method you choose depends on how urgent the task is and how high your confidence is in the team process. For a shorter project, you might pick whomever can build the team to get results quickest. For a long-term team, you might lean toward the elected leader. Either way, base the choice of leader on both technical knowledge and interpersonal skill. If you're resisting the elected method because you think the team will make their choice for the wrong reasons, give members a balanced list of selection criteria so it's not a popularity contest or a long political campaign.

You might want to consider appointing a team leader pro tem for several months. Select a temporary leader who doesn't want the glory and announces at the start that he or she will give up the responsibility later. A team that's around long enough can choose a more permanent leader when members know better what the job demands.

CASE STUDY: ABC Decision

At the end of the awareness training session, Chris and the Team Steering Council worked out a compromise. A new employee, Lynn, recently started as ABC's first sales rep. Since the sales department needs to be represented on the marketing team, adding Lynn to the team should be easy. Because Chris and Lynn worked closely together at a previous company, Chris thought that Lynn would help keep the novice marketers on the team focused. Chris received Team Steering Council support to propose Lynn as temporary marketing team leader for two to three months. Then Lynn's job would require extensive travel so the team could reevaluate the leader role without anyone losing face. Fortunately, Lynn was readily accepted because of obviously superior qualifications.

TEAM FACILITATOR

A team facilitator is the group process consultant who coaches the team leader, advises the team sponsor on team dynamics and trains the team to use team methods and improvement tools.

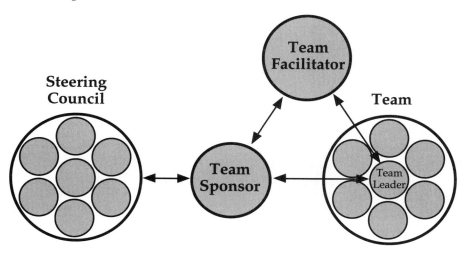

It doesn't matter much whether you recruit a team facilitator who is full-time (handling six to 10 teams), part-time (10%–20% of their time), or an outside consultant. What matters to the speed of team results is that the team facilitator is trained in group dynamics and team tools, attends all team meetings, meets frequently with the team leader and:

- Observes
- Advises
- Responds
- Explains
- Helps
- Guides
- Coaches
- Assists

- Trains
- Models
- Mentors
- Demonstrates
- Delegates
- Wears hats only temporarily
- Works through the team leader
- Remains neutral and objective

The best team facilitators don't:

- Work in the chain of command under which the team operates

- Contribute technical expertise

- Act as an actual team member

- Give project opinions or discuss content areas

- Decide for the team

- Meet with team members individually unless requested

- Run the team's project

When you recruit a team facilitator, look for someone with an impartial attitude who communicates well, understands group dynamics, runs effective meetings, gives constructive feedback and builds people's self-confidence.

Team Facilitator Functions

The specific functions of a team facilitator include:

- ▶ **Team Trainer.** Help assess training needs, create development plans, identify outside resources, conduct workshops and provide just-in-time training

- ▶ **Team Leader's Coach.** Meet before and after each team meeting to debrief, reinforce, advise, troubleshoot and plan for improvements in upcoming meetings

- ▶ **Team-Building Guide.** Suggest team-building actions, demonstrate new tools, clarify mechanics, facilitate initial discussions and mediate differences if asked

- ▶ **Team Process Consultant.** Observe group dynamics, give feedback, encourage self-monitoring, advise about long-term growth and intervene only if essential.

CASE STUDY: *News From ABC*

As a result of the awareness training, Chris decided that much of the problem with starting up the marketing team was lack of experience with the team process. So Chris recruited an equipment technician in the company, Pat, with enough experience to serve as team facilitator. As a result of Terry's encouragement, Pat's boss agreed to allocate 25 percent of Pat's time during the next three months to facilitating the marketing team.

EXERCISE: *Team Leadership*

Let's apply what we've covered to your Case Study Team.

1. What are the most important criteria for your leader?

_____

_____

2. Will you appoint the Case Study Team leader or would it be best for the team to select their own?

_____

_____

3. If appointed, who would you select?

_____

_____

4. Who will you try to recruit to serve as Case Study Team facilitator?

_____

_____

5. What skills and expertise qualify this person as team facilitator?

_____

_____

P A R T

II

Organizing
Your Team

TEAM RECRUITMENT

We've defined the support and leadership roles that a team needs, but what about our real target? A team member is an active participant who has a stake in the team's mission, shares responsibility for the team's work, conducts experiments and gathers data before team meetings, contributes information during meetings and represents the team to customers and co-workers.

Teams report that they desire team members who are:

- knowledgeable
- committed
- dependable
- vocal, open, honest
- involved
- supportive

- cooperative
- good listeners
- trusting
- hard workers
- flexible
- enthusiastic

Team members need to:

► **SHARE THE TEAM'S WORK**

Contribute to team charter and plans, share responsibility, perform their roles, follow the plan and help solve problems

► **REPRESENT THE TEAM**

Keep outsiders informed, make frequent contacts, collect customer input and participate in presentations

► **PREPARE TO CONTRIBUTE**

Get trained, read minutes, complete action items, gather information, meet with the team leader and be ready for meetings

► **PARTICIPATE IN MEETINGS**

Attend all meetings on time, participate fully, offer special expertise, listen, communicate openly, follow ground rules and work for consensus

TEAM RECRUITMENT (continued)

Team Member Selection

It's important to choose the right team members. The Team Selection Flowchart can help.

Start with a clear mission statement so you know what you want the team to accomplish. Establish key qualifications and characteristics for team personnel. Selection criteria come in three S categories.

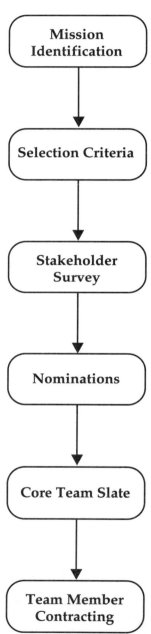

▶ *Skill:* Job knowledge and technical expertise unique to a special discipline

▶ *Style:* Personal approach, attitude, motivation, communication and group skills that affect trust, cooperation and compatibility

▶ *Stake:* Vested interest or sense of ownership resulting from personal interest, job needs, work area pressures, management priorities or performance goals

Now survey stakeholders to see who would make good team players. Stakeholders are those inside or outside the organization who have a stake in the team's work. These people include internal and external customers and suppliers; anyone involved directly in the process under study; anyone affected indirectly by the problem or situation; managers with the power to veto team recommendations and those whose support, resources or approval are needed for implementation. This is a long list, but you will save time eventually if you find out now whom you need to influence later to implement team decisions.

Nominations for your team can come from internal advertising, steering council suggestions, stakeholder requests, functional manager offers, informal volunteering, self-nomination, work group elections and personal recruitment interviews. To insure that participation is at least partially voluntary, talk to nominees and bosses early. Then you will know that they are available, interested and motivated.

If you do your homework, you'll have too many candidates to choose from. Narrow the list into a core team balanced by the three S's. A core team—those who attend all meetings and make all decisions—functions better if it includes only six to eight members. Larger team discussions become unwieldy with slower team building and postponed work progress.

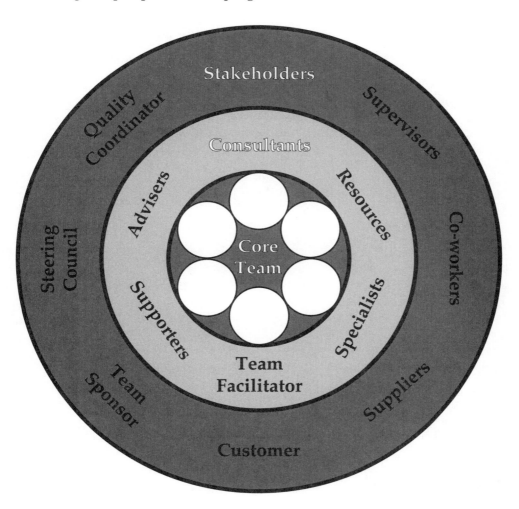

The extended team, or nonchosen stakeholders, include those whose input, expertise and support the team needs only occasionally. At meetings, members of the inner circle represent outer circle stakeholders so that all voices are heard.

TEAM RECRUITMENT (continued)

CASE STUDY: ABC Marketing Team Membership

Pat and Chris established the following criteria for membership in the marketing team.

Membership must represent all affected departments directly. Every member must:

- Understand ABC's products
- Maintain a good relationship with the co-workers they represent
- Have enough business experience to contribute to realistic decisions
- Be willing to operate with the team approach
- Commit to becoming knowledgeable in the marketing field.

At least one member needs:

- Expertise in product design and manufacture
- Knowledge of ABC's computer systems
- Practicality and task orientation
- Writing, negotiating and presenting skills.

By surveying stakeholders and networking, Pat and Chris found 17 potential members. The list included the existing five representatives from the marketing, finance, computer, manufacturing and quality control departments who attended the first meetings. The team met to agree on selection criteria; the original group decided that five other functions were missing: sales, research, engineering, materials and management. Lynn, the new temporary leader, would fill the sales hole, bringing the team to six members.

When someone suggested they recruit four more representatives, Pat said, "Ten is a large team for rapid decisions and results. Can we reduce the number without sacrificing representation?" Consequently, the computing department member agreed to work closely with research and engineering, and the manufacturing rep, who had considerable experience, agreed to speak for the materials department.

That left only the management representative. Pat suggested that the team review the membership criteria before deciding. The slate of candidates covered all criteria except the last one: writing, negotiating and presenting. Everyone acknowledged the most talented person in the company in these areas (next to the CEO) was Terry's administrative assistant, Jan. Suddenly everyone agreed that Jan should serve as their management liaison. That put the team's size at seven, which Pat felt was workable.

Contracting Team Members

Few organizations make time for the final vital recruiting step, team member contracting. A contract means a social agreement in which people agree to do something for each other. Remember, the extraordinary effort that you're hoping to get from a high-performance team is voluntary. Support begins by asking if members want to join, showing them what's in it for them, and then negotiating around their needs. Use the following worksheet as your contracting agenda.

Team Member Contracting Worksheet

RECRUITER'S BACKGROUND STATEMENTS
1. Team Mission
2. Interest in Team Member
3. Expectations of Team Member
4. Potential Rewards
QUESTIONS FOR TEAM MEMBER
5. Stake (viewpoint, job priorities, goals)
6. Style (motivation, needs, attitude)
7. Skill (resources, experience, training)
8. Concerns (questions, apprehensions, perceived obstacles)
AGREEMENTS
9. Team Role
10. Performance Expectations
11. Time Commitment
12. Boss Commitment

EXERCISE: *Team Recruitment*

Let's apply the lessons of this chapter to your Case Study Team. By following the Team Selection Flowchart, decide who should be your core team members.

CASE STUDY: Team Members

TEAM CHARTER

The members of the world's fastest teams have a sharp sense of direction and solid understanding of how their work relates to organizational goals. This understanding is achieved with a charter, which is a clear, written, agreed-upon description of the team's mission and how it relates to organizational goals, including general direction, membership and empowerment. It serves as a contract of key team mechanics among team members and between them and the team sponsor.

A team charter should be a two-way street. It defines what the team commits to do for the team sponsor and what the team sponsor agrees to do in return. Charters are constructed from answers to the following questions. Use only those elements that help unify team and sponsor.

General Direction

BACKGROUND.   Why was the team formed (include business goals, earlier similar projects, process history and customer concerns)?

MISSION.   What is the team's special assignment, role or function (define the need, system or process to be addressed and its scope and boundaries)?

ROADMAP CHOICE.   Which type of master plan is best for this mission?

DELIVERABLES.   What outcome does the team sponsor or customer expect, how will they measure success, what are the preliminary and final deadlines?

NAME.   What will the team call itself, specifying its function and primary geographic and departmental location?

Membership

STAKEHOLDERS.   Which customers must the team satisfy, which suppliers must they depend on, which team member managers and co-workers need to support it and who can influence or veto the team's decisions?

TEAM MEMBER ROLES.   Who will serve as the core team, what initial roles will they play, who will meet with which stakeholders, and who can the team call in temporarily to help?

TEAM SPONSOR ROLE.   What will the manager commit to do for the team and what functions will the team sponsor perform during and between team meetings?

Empowerment

TEAM DUTIES.   What activities will the team be expected to do?

AUTHORITY LEVEL.   What power does the team have (include what they can directly control and what needs approval in what way)?

RESOURCES.   What budget, supplies, staff time, training, space, equipment and facilities will the organization allocate to the team?

REPORTING.   What written reports, individual contacts, checkpoints, reviews and formal presentations will the team give to whom how often, and which will they receive from whom and when?

REWARDS.   How will the team be rewarded, how will team members be recognized for their contributions and what rewards will happen at which milestones?

ABC's Marketing Team Charter

Here's the charter that the ABC marketing team developed.

BACKGROUND	The modern world operates as a global economic village. Voice recognition and microchip technology provide tremendous opportunities to bridge language barriers. ABC has developed the vision and technical expertise to affect cross-cultural communication, but its nonprofit operating status did little to develop employee business skills, marketing savvy or result-oriented teamwork.
MISSION	Establish a distribution system to meet internal needs that will get ABC's future products into the hands of customers as quickly and economically as possible.
ROADMAP	New process development roadmap.
DELIVERABLES	In six months, ABC will show increasing shipments of its three key products to U.S. and European distributors based on graphs of number and value of units shipped.
NAME	Distribution Team (renamed from marketing team).

STAKEHOLDERS

- Marketing
- Manufacturing
- Materials
- Computer lab
- Equipment suppliers
- Past funding sources
- Top management

- Sales
- Engineering
- Research
- Quality control
- Manufacturers' reps
- Finance
- End customers

TEAM MEMBER ROLES

Lynn, sales rep = temporary team leader.

Marketing, finance, computer, manufacturing, quality control, management representatives = team members.

Pat, equipment tech = team facilitator.

TEAM SPONSOR ROLES   Chris agrees to full briefing of team and access to information, guidance, timely feedback on proposals, addressing roadblocks, championing team to senior management, troubleshooting team members' managers commitment.

DUTIES   *3 hours/week:* attend two team meetings

6 hours/week: collect data, meet stakeholders, solve problems

Monthly: informal progress report

As needed: document findings, make proposals to distributors, make presentations to management

AUTHORITY LEVEL   Without requesting approval, the team can:

- Collect data
- Charter satellite projects
- Manage its budget and make budgeted purchases
- Draft contracts and working arrangements
- Contact internal customers and internal/ external suppliers
- Discuss potential agreements with outside representatives
- Establish metrics to monitor existing practices

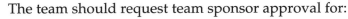

The team should request team sponsor approval for:

- Procedure changes that increase nonteam labor
- Finalizing distributor relationships
- Modifications to supplier relationships
- Committing ABC to any contractual obligations
- Recommendations containing substantial risk to customers
- Expenditures exceeding team sponsor's spending limit

ABC's Marketing Team Charter (continued)

RESOURCES

Team members' time commitment: approximately 20%

Training: Team Kick-Off Workshop, team facilitator just-in-time sessions, quarterly planning retreats, other as needed

Equipment: dedicated computer, other to be determined

Technical support: available on normal channels

Facilities: scheduled meeting room, reserved wall space

Supplies: team notebook, team kit, flip-chart

Budget: to be determined after long-range plan approval

REPORTING

- Weekly meeting minutes to team sponsor
- Biweekly team sponsor/team leader meetings
- Monthly team sponsor informal progress presentation
- Milestone completion presentations to Team Steering Council
- Stakeholder reports: to be determined in long-range plan

REWARDS

- Free meal tickets at the end of each roadmap step
- $100 bonus for completing major deliverables on time
- Team input to individual performance reviews
- All contributors to team success will receive choice follow-on assignments to further their careers

TEAM CHARTER DEVELOPMENT

Theoretically it would be nice to clarify all charter components immediately. In the real world of pressures, deadlines and limited resources, that rarely happens. It's better if management limits its involvement to specifying the minimum sense of direction so the team can find its own solutions. Here's the suggested RTD program for developing a team charter.

► **Requirements.** Define initial requirements for the team. If a steering council exists, be sure the team's goals align with its business goals and priorities.

► **Recruitment.** Recruit a team facilitator and possibly a team leader. Work with them to recruit core team members.

► **Draft M.R.D.C.** Draft critical parts of the team charter using the M.R.D.C. rule of thumb. Mission, Roadmap, and Deliverables are specific charter components. Include the fourth, Constraints, if you or the team's customer need to dictate any other boundaries, limits, deadlines or requirements.

► **Briefing.** Brief the core team on its requirements and your M.R.D.C. draft. Since information determines power, any other background you can give will help.

► *Chartering Retreat.* Host a chartering retreat, including any basic training, during which members discuss, negotiate and complete the parts of the charter they deem important. (An intensive two- to three-day session provides the fastest team deployment.)

► **Negotiate.** Let the team present its proposed charter and agree to as much as you possibly can. Negotiate adjustments where essential, but be careful not to dampen their enthusiasm and sense of ownership.

Like other contracts, a team charter should be both binding and flexible. As a living document, refer to it regularly and adjust it when needed. Tie up loose ends from the chartering retreat before too long. Occasional charter review keeps the team's sense of purpose alive and its actions focused, and when major changes occur, it provides a simple basis for renegotiation.

Why Bother?

Management needs to turn over some power to rapidly deploy a team, but contrary to frequent objections, a team sponsor shouldn't abdicate total responsibility to a team. A team charter helps management set limits, define boundaries and specify accountability. Don't confuse a charter with a plan: Soon you'll discover how a team generates its own detailed metrics, sequence of milestones and timelines.

BRIEFING THE TEAM

The better you prepare any project, the faster you can expect to get it off the ground. This rule applies strongly to teams, especially new ones. What can you tell them at the outset that will accelerate their team-building? Some answers are obvious: mission, deliverables, background, rewards and other key charter components. Others may not be so obvious.

How to Brief the Team

To empower a team quickly, you have to brief them fully at the outset and then keep them fully informed. Give members the background to understand the big picture, customer requirements and any relevant history.

Which of the following do you have information about and could brief the forming team about swiftly? Which do they need to know to make rapid progress? Which of these might they want to know about?

☐ Customer requirements	☐ Time constraints
☐ Customer feedback and satisfaction	☐ Money limitations
☐ Competitive pressures	☐ Union agreements
☐ Problem symptoms	☐ Regulatory requirements
☐ Process behavior	☐ Safety considerations
☐ Process history	☐ Labor or overtime constraints
☐ Production statistics	☐ Equipment/facility availability
☐ Financial performance	☐ Technology development
☐ Stakeholder involvement	☐ Senior management vision
☐ Earlier similar projects	☐ Driving business needs
☐ Related current efforts	☐ Strategic goals and objectives

If you put a checkmark in each square, you're right!

For the swiftest team-building, put together a presentation based on these and then follow these disclosure guidelines.

Recommended	Not Recommended
Complete information	Secrets
Full background data	Delay bad news
Trust the team	Protect their feelings
Confidentiality ground rules	The need-to-know rule
Define boundaries	Leave direction fuzzy
Agree on resources (time, money, facilities, equipment, space)	Wait and see
Train the team to understand	Hide financial and political details

ROADMAPS

Different kinds of teamwork require different approaches. Enter, the team's road-map. A roadmap tells a team how to get where it wants to go by providing a step-by-step master plan that outlines the best route to follow for that type of work. A roadmap lays out the important actions that similar previous teams used to achieve success. It functions like a seasoned scout who steers a novice trekking into the wilderness. The right roadmap provides a tested method that insures even first-time teams won't omit essential actions.

With a logical order of approaching their assignment defined in advance, a team can plan and act quickly. Roadmaps carve up overwhelming tasks into con-frontable chunks, provide defined milestones, suggest accepted tools and make it easier to hold teams accountable without too much stress. Additional benefits of using a team roadmap include:

- Prevents continual firefighting without long-term progress

- Provides a framework for easy reporting and recognition

- Allows easily understandable documents to preserve history

Roadmap Types

The table on page 61 explains the most common categories of project teams from the simplest to the most complex, each of which uses a different roadmap. Note that self-directed work groups and management teams employ different roadmaps that aren't included here.

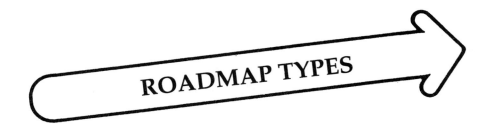

Roadmap Types

TYPE	PURPOSE	MAIN ROADMAP ACTIONS
Task Team	*Implement a specific, short-term action*	Plan approach to assignment Implement action steps Check progress and adjust accordingly Report completion
Problem Solving	*Eradicate an undesirable, unpredictable, unworkable situation*	Analyze recurring symptoms Correct underlying troubles Find and eliminate the root cause
Process Improvement	*Optimize results and control a specific, stable process that's working*	Improve productivity and yield Increase customer satisfaction Reduce waste Standardize methods Control and stabilize the process
New Product/ Process	*Develop and introduce a new product or process*	Do research and benchmark technology Examine methods and consider options Design or reengineer process Plan and conduct experiments Pilot, expand and standardize process

A brief description of each roadmap follows. The first roadmap has the narrowest scope and, all other things being equal, will produce the quickest results, but considering your ultimate goals, is task implementation enough? Maybe the patience for a longer-term approach will provide greater payoff eventually.

TASK/IMPLEMENTATION TEAM ROADMAP

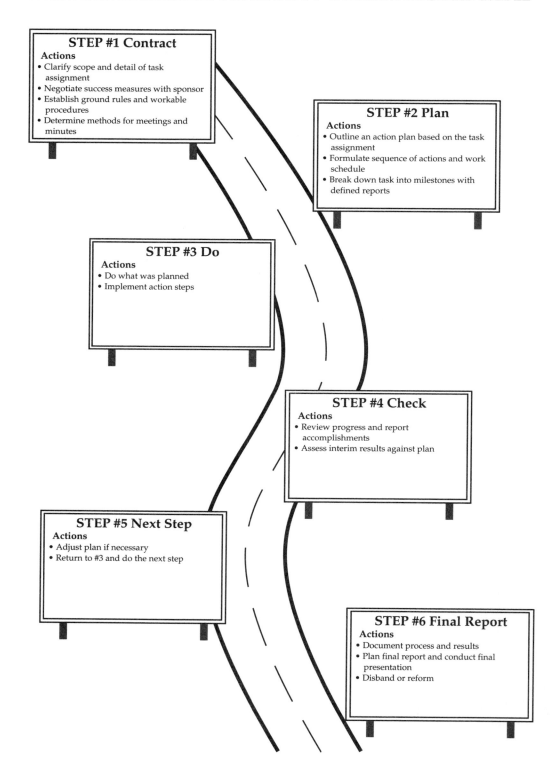

STEP #1 Contract

Actions
- Clarify scope and detail of task assignment
- Negotiate success measures with sponsor
- Establish ground rules and workable procedures
- Determine methods for meetings and minutes

STEP #2 Plan

Actions
- Outline an action plan based on the task assignment
- Formulate sequence of actions and work schedule
- Break down task into milestones with defined reports

STEP #3 Do

Actions
- Do what was planned
- Implement action steps

STEP #4 Check

Actions
- Review progress and report accomplishments
- Assess interim results against plan

STEP #5 Next Step

Actions
- Adjust plan if necessary
- Return to #3 and do the next step

STEP #6 Final Report

Actions
- Document process and results
- Plan final report and conduct final presentation
- Disband or reform

PROBLEM-SOLVING ROADMAP

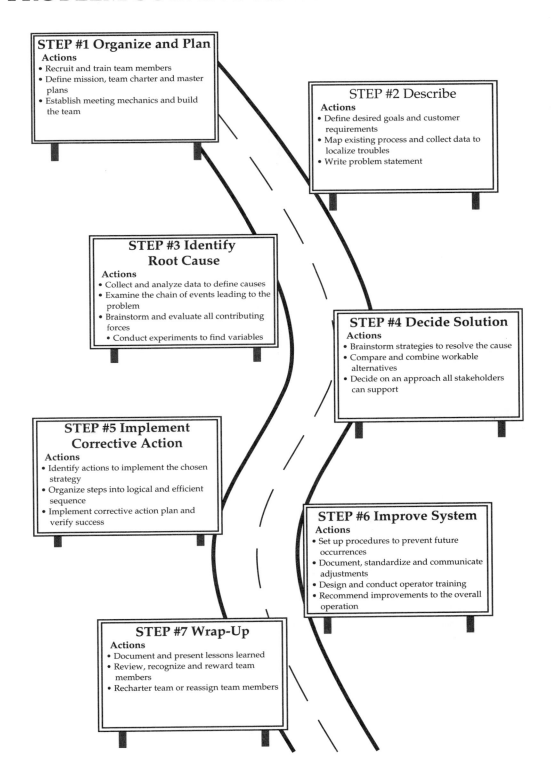

STEP #1 Organize and Plan

Actions
- Recruit and train team members
- Define mission, team charter and master plans
- Establish meeting mechanics and build the team

STEP #2 Describe

Actions
- Define desired goals and customer requirements
- Map existing process and collect data to localize troubles
- Write problem statement

STEP #3 Identify Root Cause

Actions
- Collect and analyze data to define causes
- Examine the chain of events leading to the problem
- Brainstorm and evaluate all contributing forces
- Conduct experiments to find variables

STEP #4 Decide Solution

Actions
- Brainstorm strategies to resolve the cause
- Compare and combine workable alternatives
- Decide on an approach all stakeholders can support

STEP #5 Implement Corrective Action

Actions
- Identify actions to implement the chosen strategy
- Organize steps into logical and efficient sequence
- Implement corrective action plan and verify success

STEP #6 Improve System

Actions
- Set up procedures to prevent future occurrences
- Document, standardize and communicate adjustments
- Design and conduct operator training
- Recommend improvements to the overall operation

STEP #7 Wrap-Up

Actions
- Document and present lessons learned
- Review, recognize and reward team members
- Recharter team or reassign team members

PROCESS IMPROVEMENT ROADMAP

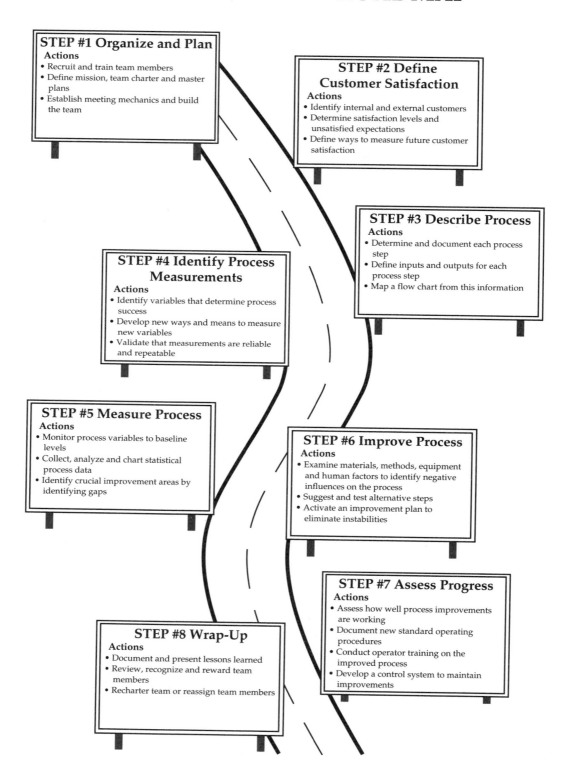

STEP #1 Organize and Plan
Actions
- Recruit and train team members
- Define mission, team charter and master plans
- Establish meeting mechanics and build the team

STEP #2 Define Customer Satisfaction
Actions
- Identify internal and external customers
- Determine satisfaction levels and unsatisfied expectations
- Define ways to measure future customer satisfaction

STEP #3 Describe Process
Actions
- Determine and document each process step
- Define inputs and outputs for each process step
- Map a flow chart from this information

STEP #4 Identify Process Measurements
Actions
- Identify variables that determine process success
- Develop new ways and means to measure new variables
- Validate that measurements are reliable and repeatable

STEP #5 Measure Process
Actions
- Monitor process variables to baseline levels
- Collect, analyze and chart statistical process data
- Identify crucial improvement areas by identifying gaps

STEP #6 Improve Process
Actions
- Examine materials, methods, equipment and human factors to identify negative influences on the process
- Suggest and test alternative steps
- Activate an improvement plan to eliminate instabilities

STEP #7 Assess Progress
Actions
- Assess how well process improvements are working
- Document new standard operating procedures
- Conduct operator training on the improved process
- Develop a control system to maintain improvements

STEP #8 Wrap-Up
Actions
- Document and present lessons learned
- Review, recognize and reward team members
- Recharter team or reassign team members

NEW PRODUCT/PROCESS ROADMAP

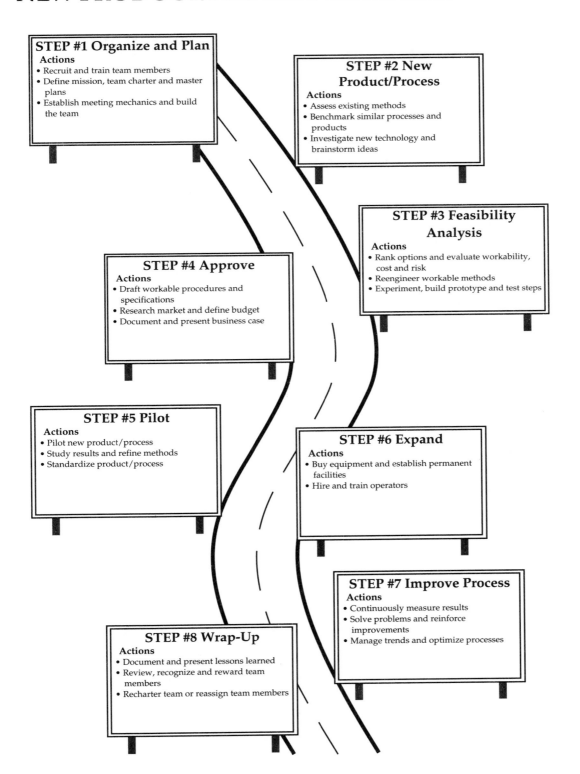

STEP #1 Organize and Plan

Actions
- Recruit and train team members
- Define mission, team charter and master plans
- Establish meeting mechanics and build the team

STEP #2 New Product/Process

Actions
- Assess existing methods
- Benchmark similar processes and products
- Investigate new technology and brainstorm ideas

STEP #3 Feasibility Analysis

Actions
- Rank options and evaluate workability, cost and risk
- Reengineer workable methods
- Experiment, build prototype and test steps

STEP #4 Approve

Actions
- Draft workable procedures and specifications
- Research market and define budget
- Document and present business case

STEP #5 Pilot

Actions
- Pilot new product/process
- Study results and refine methods
- Standardize product/process

STEP #6 Expand

Actions
- Buy equipment and establish permanent facilities
- Hire and train operators

STEP #7 Improve Process

Actions
- Continuously measure results
- Solve problems and reinforce improvements
- Manage trends and optimize processes

STEP #8 Wrap-Up

Actions
- Document and present lessons learned
- Review, recognize and reward team members
- Recharter team or reassign team members

EXERCISE: Team Briefing

1. Review the requirements you established for your Case Study Team. Assuming you're the team sponsor, define the minimum sense of direction you would provide using the M.R.D.C. formula. (If none of the generic roadmaps fit, design your own.)

   Mission

   _____

   _____

   _____

   Roadmap Choice

   _____

   _____

   _____

   Deliverables

   _____

   _____

   _____

   Constraints

   _____

   _____

   _____

2. Plan an agenda to brief the team so that they would start off with essential information.

   _____

   _____

   _____

MASTER PLANNING

Teams need a simple way to overcome the natural tendency to work at cross purposes that's typical of most people with different personalities, backgrounds and styles. With good plans developed in common, teams are much more likely to:

- Stay focused on priorities

- Support a unified approach

- Coordinate action to avoid inefficiency

- Measure progress and maintain accountability

Although plans, once implemented, may need to be refocused, teams gain knowledge and control through planning which allows them to adjust their path midstream when needed.

Strategic Planning

What kind of planning are we talking about? Although a team charter is a needed element, its long-term view isn't enough. What's missing from most teams' repertoires, as the following table shows, is a master plan that links purposes at the top with day-to-day activities at the bottom. A master plan keeps teams focused and forces them to measure short-term progress. The three stages form a strategic plan.

PHASE	CONTENTS	METHODS
Team Charter	General direction that identifies critical issues needing work	• Organizational goals • Business strategies
Master Plans	Milestones for each roadmap step with deadlines	• Long-range project plans • Objectives and deliverables
Action Plans	Specific work targets that define who will do what by when	• Short-range plans • Team workplans

The team roadmap is our secret weapon that makes it easy to establish two or three milestones for each roadmap step. That's the best way to develop a master plan. Look at ABC's Distribution Team master plan based on the new process roadmap on page 68.

MASTER PLANNING (continued)

ABC Distribution Team Master Plan

STEP 1: Organize and Plan

Milestones

- Get team sponsor sign-off on complete mission, team charter and master plan by week 1
- Publish ground rules and meeting mechanics to maximize team efficiency by week 2

STEP 2: New Process

Milestones

- Issue a report that measures similar distribution processes used in related industries by week 5
- Get Team Steering Council commitment on preferred product distribution scheme for ABC by week 6

STEP 3: Feasibility Analysis

Milestones

- Document proposed distribution scheme including process step description, flowchart and specifications by week 7
- Locate and secure letter of intent from qualified outside manufacturers' representatives by week 9
- Publish cost analysis comparing internal versus external distribution scheme by week 10

STEP 4: Approve

Milestones

- Present business case to all internal stakeholders and secure approval of proposed distribution scheme from top management by week 12

STEP 5: Pilot

Milestones

- Pilot new product distribution process by week 14

- Standardize distribution process through continuous improvement and publish working procedures by week 18

STEP 6: Expand

Milestones

- Monitor the interaction between affected departments using weekly production charts as deliveries expand from week 18 until 26

STEP 7: Improve Process

Milestones

- Solve all distribution problems that arise within one week

- Run experiments to optimize the efficiency of forecasting and distribution processes until the returns from improvements diminish to minimal levels

STEP 8: Wrap-Up

Milestones

- Report lessons learned at a final Team Steering Council presentation by week 36

- Reassign team members to new teams that can benefit from their experience

HOW TO PLAN

If you ask most teams to brainstorm what they need to do, everything will tumble out, including mission, goals, inputs, outputs, war stories, actions, complaints, objectives, past failures. It won't look anything like the diagram that shows an organized master under the umbrella of the team charter. But if you get the team to arrange and group their answers under the appropriate roadmap steps, order appears quickly.

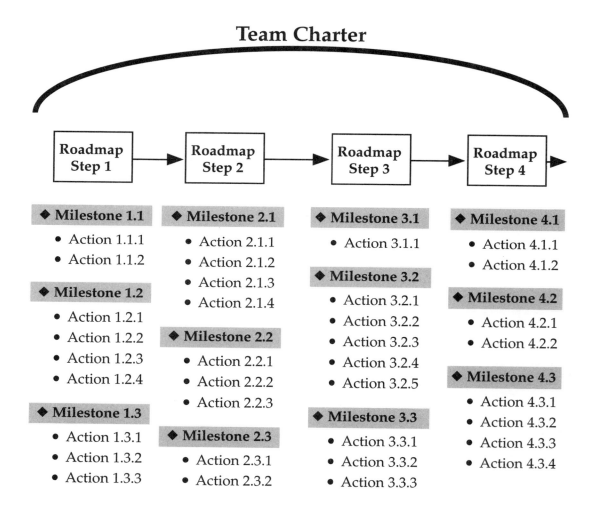

If the team's brainstorming is typical, they may have 20 or 30 actions listed under each roadmap step. With further thought and analysis they could categorize each roadmap step's actions under two or three major accomplishments or deliverables.

To speed both planning and implementation, you need the team to distinguish inputs from outputs and start thinking in terms of milestones. Milestones are midrange targets that reduce a large task into smaller but challenging chunks of output. A team uses them to pace itself, show how far it has to go and create a sense of progress. Once the categories under each roadmap step are clear, they get turned into milestones by using the same SMART Worksheet we used for deliverables on page 26.

Master Planning Flowchart

The following flowchart describes this process in more detail.

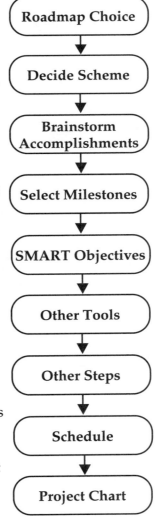

1. Select or design the appropriate roadmap during team charter development.

2. Decide if you will develop milestones for roadmap steps separately or all at once.

3. Brainstorm major outcomes and critical deliverables needed to accomplish the whole plan or roadmap step.

4. Evaluate the list, identify priority deliverables and select one to three per step to serve as milestones.

5. Define each milestone as a SMART objective (specific, measurable, agreed, result-oriented and time-bound).

6. Adjust milestones by planning for contingencies, training, public relations and recognition.

7. Repeat the above for other roadmap steps or attach milestones to appropriate roadmap steps.

8. Establish a schedule by correlating milestone timeframes and charter deliverables.

9. Rewrite your plan into one clear document and map out a project tracking diagram.

EXERCISE: Master Planning

1. Review your Case Study Team's mission, charter components and roadmap choice.

2. Use the roadmap descriptions to brainstorm accomplishments for each step. Record your ideas on the Master Planning Worksheet.

3. Categorize, combine, cut and edit your list to give you the minimum major accomplishments necessary to complete each roadmap step.

4. Refine initial ideas into discreet milestones with the SMART Worksheet.

Master Planning Worksheet

Roadmap Step	#	SMART Milestones
	1.	
	2.	
	3.	
	4.	
	5.	
	6.	
	7.	
	8.	

PRESENTING THE PLAN

Team presentations are a great opportunity to accelerate growth or kill empowerment. Part of the team deal includes doing everything possible to see that they succeed. Here are some presentation ground rules based on the principle that the team sponsor who has to say no to the team has screwed up:

- Don't drop in uninvited

- Follow the team's meeting ground rules

- Give positive reinforcement whenever and wherever possible

- Search for things to agree with

- Give advice when the team needs and wants coaching

- Be flexible in adjusting plans and renegotiating the team's charter

In spite of your best efforts, if the team comes up with impractical proposals, then:

- Respond carefully

- Find something to agree with to say yes instead of no

- Identify the missing information for briefing or training the team

- Coach the team on how to make their proposals acceptable

Other Planning Tools

This planning method takes only a few hours and can save endless false starts and delays later. While it's a good investment, you might think that, instead of planning, the team could have been working. A team should make only plans that will help it stabilize and speed progress, but remember the basic rule of architecture: Form follows function. Use only those planning tools that team functions require. With that in mind, let's consider two other team functions that can become major obstacles to RTD if not addressed early: politics and motivation.

TEAM PUBLIC RELATIONS

Build the team's image and credibility with customers, suppliers and stakeholders and head off politics at the pass. How many great ideas go down the tubes because they weren't communicated persuasively? A team should think of itself as a network hub that spreads the gospel it develops. A Team PR Plan should include:

► **Deciding Desired Image.** How outsiders should view the team so that they'll value what is produced and support implementation

► **Segmenting Stakeholders.** Carving up outside circles of interested parties and assigning team member representatives to stay in touch

► **Designing Campaigns.** Deciding what messages to spread, what information to broadcast and how all this will happen

► **Establishing Reports.** Planning who should get team minutes and other documents how often

Following through on a Team PR Plan makes good business sense. The team will get valuable input to incorporate into their work. They'll keep their supporters in the loop enough to keep supplying resources. They'll discover related changes while there's still time to respond, and they'll surface key objections early enough to solve them.

Team Recognition

The other obstacle that retards team acceleration is member motivation. If you've done your team sponsor homework, the team should be enthusiastic, but the fledgling team needs to know that you'll stay behind them. You need to convince them that management support won't dry up when another possibly lucrative pet rock comes by.

That's where recognition comes in. People tend to repeat behavior that's rewarded. Recognition is not just the compliments you pay them when they do something right or the bonuses or promotions they earn after the project is over.

Examine any high-performance team and you'll find that they party often, celebrate all successes and have lots of fun together. And this doesn't slow them down. On the contrary, the climate that's created fuels acceleration.

For RTD to work, you need a motivational system that's simple to operate, consistent and fair, routinely practiced instead of forgotten, frequent enough to reward small wins, based on team achievement and under the team's control. How's that last one for truly practicing empowerment?

How To Do It

Try the following process. Ask the team to plan the rewards they'll earn when delivering on their promises. Give them guidelines such as:

✔ At the accomplishment of defined milestones or special effort, team members will be recognized with one of the following awards worth $15:

- breakfast, lunch, or ice cream social
- movie tickets
- engraved trinket (key chain, mouse pad)
- team T-shirt or hat

✔ At the accomplishment of major team goals, all team members will be recognized with one or more of the following awards worth $25–$100:

- dinner and sporting event for two
- newsletter/newspaper article
- sweatshirt/gift certificate
- framed certificate from CEO

To qualify, a team submits its master plan with defined rewards for its planned milestones. Funding for these rewards gets built into the budget. Management can set controls to insure the goodies are affordable, and the team is guaranteed they won't be forgotten.

This reward system skirts the larger issue of how team contributions get reflected in promotions and performance reviews. You'll encourage team-building by shifting incentives throughout your organization from individual to collective.

P A R T

III

Team-Building
Dynamics

TEAM KICK-OFF

Team-building can include:

- Joint Planning

- Interactive Training Sessions

- Consensus Decision-Making

- Motivation and Incentive Programs

- Reorganizing Around Self-Directed Work

- Developing Cross-Functional Partnerships

- Experiential Events (Like Wilderness Ropes Courses)

- Group Problem-Solving and Conflict Resolution

- Getting to Know Each Other Through Games and Social Events

When we started, we reviewed the stages of team development—forming, storming and norming—that lead to performing. Now we will delve more into this progression and discover how to accelerate team progress. Remember, these stages are natural. We can do only so much to hasten each team member's ability to adjust, accept, learn, trust and cooperate, but we'll learn how to use tools that enhance team-building and how to avoid pitfalls that impede development.

We're studying team-building, the third stage of the team lifecycle, after the organizing stage. In reality, they should happen concurrently. Give team members the freedom to do things their own way during briefing, chartering and planning, and they will develop into a coordinated working unit sooner.

TEAM KICK-OFF (continued)

The Forming Stage

"Forming" stage teams tend to be:

- Unclear and uncertain about what to do and how to behave

- Polite and quiet with cautious participation

- Unfamiliar, tentative, hesitant, anxious or suspicious

- Interested only superficially, with little in-depth listening

- Worried about making a contribution and concerned about getting hurt

- Ambivalent but dependent on the team leader or dominant personality

- Uncommitted with little attachment and little work accomplished

Because these characteristics are human nature, there's no guarantee that a forming team will start off on the right foot. You won't break any RTD records if you have to abort because few members show up for meetings, no one knows what to do or everyone argues.

The following table suggests four categories of tools to help form a team: brief them, encourage them to bond into a cohesive unit, involve them wherever possible and empower them as much as they're ready for.

Accelerating Forming Stage Team-Building

(Briefing)

- Hold a kick-off briefing

- Give full background information

- Answer all questions forthrightly

- Create a clear-cut sense of direction

- Present team mission, goals and requirements

- Identify outputs and deliverables needed from the team

- Define tasks, responsibilities and individual contributions

- Provide training on team roles, tools and basic processes

(Bonding)

- Make team members feel welcome and needed

- Develop relationships to unify team members

- Help the team learn about each others' background and skills

- Schedule a tour of each team member's work area

- Teach them to work through each other's personal style

- Establish ground rules to develop common ground

- Insure that personal goals will be achieved through the team

- Encourage team members to connect

- Build mutual trust between members, team and management

TEAM KICK-OFF (continued)

Involvement

- Use warm-up exercises to focus energy

- Challenge the team to get involved

- Introduce activities to demonstrate cooperation

- Cultivate participation with communication

- Encourage creativity, accept feedback and capture all input

- Generate new ideas about team charter and plans

- Brainstorm problems and their causes

- Address initial concerns honestly and flexibly

Empowerment

- Let the team finalize its charter

- Have the team develop a master plan

- Let the team run meetings as soon as possible

- Guide the team to distribute their workload

- Identify expectations to uncover common goals

- Encourage and facilitate consensus decision making

- Delegate decisions about priorities to the team

- Help the team to resolve conflicts on its own

You don't have to do everything on this list—use only the tools that the team needs for rapid growth. Maybe you'll be lucky and find that the human side of team formation happens on its own during organizing activities, but in case it doesn't, we will look at the one group we've ignored so far: bonding.

BONDING TEAMS

To function as a team, individuals must bond into a cohesive unit. The ties that members develop start with personal contact, grow into stronger connections as team members work together and ultimately create a solid union when trust and respect develop.

Sometimes just throwing all the right pieces together isn't enough. Team members often have serious questions such as:

✔ Will I be accepted and needed?

✔ What will I have to give up if I join?

✔ Who will be in charge and hold what power?

✔ Will my voice be heard?

✔ Will my contributions be valued?

✔ How concerned is the team for my welfare?

If these questions aren't answered, cooperative relationships won't form.

To insure that the right answers are found quickly, many team builders allocate time early for team bonding. ABC's Distribution Team facilitator, Pat, suggested that they plan some work area tours, group dynamics exercises, outside social activities, personal style workshops, meeting warm-ups and kick-off training so that team members could get to know each other better and forge new partnerships. Chris understood the general intent, but didn't see the benefit in many of these suggestions. We'll discuss four bonding methods that have the highest leverage on team speed—communication, ground rules, training and trust building—before deciding what's best for the Distribution Team.

FOLLOW THESE COMMUNICATION GUIDELINES . . .

BONDING TEAM (continued)

Team Communication Guidelines

Communication is vital for teammates to work together smoothly. Gaps, break-downs, misunderstandings and unwillingness to open up may do more to slow teams down than any other internal factor.

Include communication skill-building exercises in initial training. Encourage teams to include these do's and don'ts in their ground rules, and then give them feedback and coaching to help them find new ways of behaving.

DO	DON'T
• Organize thoughts	• Clutter thoughts
• Assert your opinion	• Be aggressive
• Listen actively	• Block others
• Be open	• Close your mind
• Respond	• Resist

This communicating style is a *definite* DON'T!

TEAM GROUND RULES

When a team first gets together, neither new teammates nor seasoned veterans automatically know the best way to act toward each other. The smart thing to do is to develop a tailored set of team ground rules, which are statements of basic values that a team establishes to serve as behavioral guidelines so that individual team members know how to interact and support each other. You can use them to standardize procedure, time management, work assignments, logistics, preparation, discussion, creativity, reporting, respect, courtesy and problem-solving. The following worksheet helps.

Team Ground Rules Worksheet

GROUND RULE CATEGORY	TEAM GROUND RULES
Respect.　How team members should work together, treat each other; handle rank, equality, confidentiality, recognition and courtesy	
Responsibility.　How team members will delegate assignments and distribute action items	
Procedures.　How the team will plan, record and report its work; set priorities, handle changes and make decisions	
Discussion.　How team members will participate, communicate and give feedback	
Differences.　How the team will handle disagreements and criticism	
Schedule.　When the team will meet and for how long; how it will regulate attendance, promptness, breaks and interruptions	
Meetings.　How the team will prepare agendas, judge a quorum, respond to absences and replacements, handle interruptions and tangents, document minutes	
Work Management.　How the team will manage its project, monitor progress, stay on track, report success and problems, represent status to outsiders	
Non-Team Behavior.　How the team will improve poor motivation or attitude, ignored action items, smoking, inappropriate behavior or language	

TEAM GROUND RULES (continued)

A new team should define its most obvious ground rules as soon as possible. If the team follows the rules of brainstorming, lots of ideas, good and bad, will surface. The team should go over the list and decide which are the minimum essentials. Don't expect a team to cover every conceivable issue at the start. Just publish the list and post it on a chart for reference during all team meetings.

CASE STUDY: ABC Distribution Team Ground Rules

ABC's Distribution Team established the following initial ground rules.

- **Leave Your Rank At the Door**

- **All Ideas Are Valuable**

- **Listen with Respect As An Ally**

- **All for One and One for All**

- **Share Everything Equally**

- **Use Consensus Wherever Possible**

- **Attack Problems, Not People**

- **Complete Your Action Items**

Good ground rules are clear, consistent, agreed to, reinforced and followed, so encourage everyone to take them seriously. As the team progresses, they can revise them in response to unexpected situations, problems or awareness of what's necessary for success. Keep the list visible. If ground rules work as planned, the team's connections will get stronger as they take charge of their own relationships.

TEAM TRAINING

A powerful bonding experience often happens in team training. When new teams work together, they learn what they need to do, how to operate in unison and how to use new team tools. They discover how to work better together than they would have separately. Team training involves:

► **TEAM BUILDING SKILLS**

How to define roles, share responsibility, encourage participation, structure cooperation, establish ground rules, conduct warm-ups and work through differences

► **ORGANIZING SKILLS**

How to develop a mission statement, team charter, roadmap, master plan, short-range action plans, budgets, schedule and PR plans

► **PEOPLE SKILLS**

How to listen actively, communicate clearly, lead, coach, train, negotiate, present to groups, resolve conflicts and troubleshoot problems

► **MEETING SKILLS**

How to organize meetings, plan agendas, moderate discussion, generate ideas, make consensus decisions, close discussions and establish action items

► **SUPPORTING TOOLS**

How to use tools to collect and analyze data, find root causes, solve problems, use statistical process controls, read charts, design roadmaps and make continuous improvements

► **WORK AND PROJECT MANAGEMENT**

How to coordinate efforts, measure quality, monitor progress, interface with stakeholders, manage finances, control costs and document actions

► **TECHNICAL SKILLS**

How to understand the systems, conduct the functions, operate the equipment and improve the processes the team is responsible for, including extensive cross-training on each other's jobs

Depending on team charter and planned investment in team performance level, decide which of these topics to include in your team's training.

TEAM TRAINING (continued)

Team Kick-Off Training

The best way to kick off an RTD team is at a multiday, off-site retreat. This way, you can address everything at once and rapid deployment of a soon-to-be high-performance team becomes possible. When a retreat isn't practical, come as close to that ideal as you can. Schedule longer and more frequent initial team meetings that include one or two hours of training each. Remember, a slow start can dramatically slow down urgently needed team results.

Here's how ABC's Distribution Team orchestrated their kick-off training at an initial off-site retreat and several follow-up meetings.

LEAD BY TEAM . . .	TOPIC	PROCESS
Facilitator	Orientation to team process	*Presentation*
Leader	Team warm-up to get to know each other	*Discussion*
Sponsor	Mission and background	*Presentation*
Facilitator	Team concepts and methods	*Training*
Leader	Setting ground rules	*Discussion*
Facilitator	Team meeting processes	*Training*
Leader	Choosing roles and rotation scheme	*Discussion*
Facilitator	Consensus decision making	*Training*
Leader	Resolve initial issues and conflicts	*Consensus*
Facilitator	Team charter components	*Training*
Leader	Team charter development	*Consensus*
Sponsor	Team charter proposal	*Negotiation*
Facilitator	Team roadmap and planning tools	*Training*
Leader	Develop master, PR and recognition plan	*Consensus*
Sponsor	Master plan proposal	*Negotiation*
Facilitator	Data collection, problem-solving, quality tools	*Training*
Leader	Action plans to accomplish first milestone	*Consensus*

Just-In-Time Team Training

The recommended agenda for team kick-off training just scratches the surface of what high-performance teams eventually master. Of course, it's impractical to teach a forming team everything they'll need to know all at once. Even if you could teach everything at one sitting, most people would forget what they don't apply immediately. So reality presents us with another critical question: How do you get to other important training while the team gets some work done?

Just-in-time training is the solution. Start the team with as much intensive training as possible. Since you'll never cover everything needed, remain alert to training gaps that occur. Respond with short sessions appropriate to what the team is working on. Midstream intensive workshops help, but 5 to 30 minute modules at the right spot can meet 80 percent of the team's remaining training needs.

Think how much faster you could deploy teams if everyone in your organization were trained on team tools and mechanics. If you're planning more teams or an entire team environment, maybe you should refocus from immediate results and consider training time and money a long-term investment.

HOW TO BREAK MUTUAL TRUST

Mutual trust between team and management is essential for high-performance teamwork. Without it, teams won't function at all. With it, the pace of team growth is sometimes startling. If

- defensiveness
- fear of failure
- ulterior motives
- hidden agendas
- self-serving behavior
- strong emotional reactions
- embarrassment in exposing feelings
- unwillingness to admit problems
- guarded speech
- judging and overt button pushing exist

then you must include building mutual trust as a team-development target.

Trust builds gradually and breaks suddenly. Once broken, it isn't easily recovered if ever. Here are some ways to cause trust to plummet downward:

▶ Changing the rules of the game midstream

▶ Holding information back

▶ Continuously looking over the team's shoulder

▶ Micromanaging and oversupervising

▶ Frequently criticizing team actions

▶ Playing politics with team resources and proposals

▶ Always playing devil's advocate on team proposals

▶ Ignoring team minutes and reports

▶ Taking no action on team proposals

▶ Not providing promised resources and rewards

▶ Rewarding nonteam players

HOW TO BUILD MUTUAL TRUST

On the plus side, the following elements contribute to building trust.

Honesty	→	Truth with integrity and without exaggerations or lies
Openness	→	Willing to listen fully and share all ideas and feelings
Consistency	→	Predictable responses and stable principles
Respect	→	Treat all people with dignity, equality and fairness
Promises	→	Team members who always keep their word without fail

Trust-Building Strategies

Use the following seven strategies to build team trust.

#1 Allocate time for team-building activities

#2 Provide ample autonomy

#3 Encourage risk taking

#4 Let communication run its full course

#5 Encourage and act on feedback from the team

#6 Help them feel secure in admitting mistakes

#7 Help the team become self-correcting

EXERCISE: *Team Training*

Consider the slate you established for your Case Study Team, the experience of the proposed members and its proposed team charter.

1. Which team-building activities would help bond this team rapidly?

   _____

   _____

   _____

2. Which ground rules will be essential for this team?

   _____

   _____

   _____

3. Plan an agenda for initial team training including any above items.

   _____

   _____

   _____

4. Decide how to schedule the team's kick-off (retreat, location, frequent meetings, timing).

   _____

   _____

   _____

HANDLING TEAM DIFFERENCES

To succeed, a team must remain focused on its overall mission. Shared goals and individual commitment to the larger good are essential. Everyone must learn to trust each other enough to work together. Unfortunately, these requirements don't automatically accompany the decision to form a team.

Storming Symptoms

If individuals' issues take higher priority than collective success, the project probably will fail. The team will be distracted, cooperation becomes difficult, morale drops, time is lost, and progress may be halted. This can happen at any point of team growth but is widespread during the storming stage, which may include the following symptoms.

- Overt challenges and disagreements
- Demands about personal concerns and independence
- Criticism, attacks and strong emotional reactions
- Jealousy and distrust of team members
- Hidden agendas, turf politics, cliques and splinter groups
- Testing leadership and control
- Stress, confusion and distractions
- Work accomplished only in fits and starts

CASE STUDY: ABC Update

After a few weeks, the ABC Distribution Team picked up speed, but then members began to argue. Some futuristic thinkers believed that the company should push the wristwatch version of their product. They felt the obvious Dick Tracy connections would catapult ABC into the public eye. More conservative team members thought that this path would create too much risk, because subminiature products are much harder to build in volume. Arguments broke out in the midst of other discussions, sapping energy and distracting the team.

Why Differences?

People are different, and since teams work hard to draw out everyone's ideas and feelings, these differences emerge quickly. Even in the most seasoned groups, conflicting positions between team members are natural and occur all the time, but you can spot an immature team by noticing its majority of unwilling, uncommitted or uncooperative members.

HANDLING TEAM DIFFERENCES (continued)

Disruptions

To prevent natural differences from disrupting team progress, good team leaders try to resolve individual issues outside of meetings. When friction is ignored or handled poorly, the team gets distracted from its work. Disruptions appear when the team feels uncomfortable, storms instead of works, gets off track, wastes time or has its progress impeded. When handled constructively, differences stimulate creativity.

When disruptions aren't handled early enough, conflict appears as total communication breakdowns, strong emotional reactions, team members quitting, personality clashes or out of control meetings.

Most teams expect the team leader to handle disruptions because the effect is cumulative. The more it happens, the worse it gets. Conflict can be a learning experience, too, but it's time consuming and energy draining. The more you can prevent conflict from happening, the faster your team will progress.

Alternatives for Handling Differences

When you accept that a team needs to learn to handle these troubles professionally, what do you do? Reacting negatively to a difference of opinion results in encouraging conformity, hampering creativity, discarding new ideas and invalidating the consensus concept. For example, the ABC Distribution Team's manufacturing member, J.R., has a strong view very different from the rest of the team. J.R. thinks that, because of the complexity of manufacture, wristwatch translator production will kill the company.

How can this situation be handled? The team can ignore, discipline or blame J.R., who probably would resent it and might get defensive. J.R. could get louder or give in and learn to keep quiet. Other team members probably wouldn't be as open in the future and lasting tension might ensue.

The Distribution Team could discuss the situation as a joint issue, try to understand J.R.'s viewpoint and find a solution that everyone, not just the majority, can live with. Respect is the key guideline and active listening is the key tool. Nobody is wrong. The team permits unusual views, which can be absorbed into the collective team mind. New ideas are encouraged, consensus occurs more rapidly and the team learns and grows.

STORMING RECOMMENDATIONS

Here are some principles your team could use to get through storming the best and fastest way.

PRINCIPLE	SUGGESTED APPLICATION
Welcome Differences	• Encourage frank expression of personal concerns • Accept all input and respect all team members' positions • Find something positive in every divergent view • Treat all feelings and opinions as belonging to the whole team • Incorporate and integrate all statements into team discussion • Document all comments in team notes and minutes • Recognize, don't avoid, frustrated team members • Insure anyone can speak openly without repercussions
React Positively	• Encourage team members to air differences • Be positive and constructive in the face of conflict • Patiently but assertively moderate discussion, including venting • Honor personal needs and advocate for individual welfare • Work to fix the problem, not the blame • Maintain and enhance individual self-esteem
Use Empathy	• Listen actively and as an ally • Acknowledge understanding before presenting alternatives • Insure everyone feels their voice is heard • Focus on others' ideas and feelings • Give teammates the benefit of the doubt • Try to see things from the other person's viewpoint • Relate similar situations that you've observed

STORMING RECOMMENDATIONS (continued)

PRINCIPLE	SUGGESTED APPLICATION
Use Positive Feedback	• Use recognition and advice instead of criticism or punishment • Use "I" statements to avoid judging and evaluating • Focus on the situation, not the person • Coach by being direct, specific, assertive, firm and helpful • Use your body language to show that others count • Balance everything you do with positive reinforcement
Confront Problems	• Explore differences by discussing all sides openly • Prevent worse problems by acting before things get serious • Find root causes, not symptoms, to find solutions • When facing problems, remember: Sooner is easier • Take personal responsibility whether it's your problem or not • Turn all conflict situations into learning opportunities
Negotiate Solutions Together	• Try to negotiate win-wins by collaborating on solutions • Encourage teammates to solve each other's problems • Facilitate group decision making by seeking consensus • Adjust mission, charter, roles and responsibilities as needed

HOW TO NEGOTIATE DIFFERENCES

Even if your team's ground rules reflect good dialogue and positive feedback, they still may run into issues that divide them. What do you do about such impasses? Negotiate. Negotiation means exchanging views to reach agreement. Teamwork demands a win-win from every disagreement, where both sides were fair to each other and walk away satisfied that each gained something.

If you had to solve a teammate's problem, you wouldn't recommend something you couldn't live with, would you? That's the team way of negotiating differences, as presented below.

Presentations — Each presents their reality while the other listens, acknowledges and interrupts only to clarify understanding. Recording comments at this point is useful. A discussion moderator may help insure that communication works.

Agreements — Both sides find, discuss and list areas of agreement, common goals, interests, values and views. Don't shortcut this step. Agreements are usually the key to resolving differences.

Differences — Identify issues of disagreement that interfere with complete agreement. Narrow the key differences to the top one or two, then discuss them in depth to understand opposing views and finally define the exact problem.

Negotiation — Discuss ways to resolve the differences, with each party trying to solve the other's problem. Consider all alternatives and evaluate strategies until you find a mutually acceptable solution for each issue. End only when you agree on implementation.

This sequence lets each party feel heard, concentrates on common goals first and uses a constructive approach to bridge any remaining gaps. If you follow this agenda, you'll be miles ahead while other teams are still arguing in your dust.

HOW TO NEGOTIATE DIFFERENCES
(continued)

CASE STUDY:
ABC Distribution's Wristwatch Resolution

Here's the negotiation agenda that ABC's Distribution Team developed to work out the difference about the wristwatch model.

Presentations Most of the team wants to produce wristwatch translators, which they think will catapult ABC into the public eye because of the appeal of the Dick Tracy connection. The other side, primarily J.R., feels that since subminiature products are much harder to produce in volume, the complexity of production could kill the company's chances for rapid growth.

Agreements Both sides want ABC to succeed and provide translators to people all over the world. They all believe they're doing the right things for the right reasons and that the potential for profit is tremendous.

Differences Unlike most other members of the team, J.R. has seen complex manufacturing processes overwhelmed by too much demand too fast. Inexperienced members of the team are fantasizing about selling hundreds of thousands of wristwatches in just a few months.

Negotiation By detailing best- and worst-case scenarios, the team realizes that they'll probably deliver thousands, not hundreds of thousands, of units until manufacturing refines its processes. J.R.'s fear abates, and the team decides to let the marketplace decide which product version should be pushed.

EXERCISE: *Negotiating Differences*

The following exercise uses this approach for negotiating differences.

1. Select a likely conflict between two members of your Case Study Team.

2. Using the Win-Win Worksheet, define the two sides of the issue.

3. Examine agreements and unwritten contracts that the two share.

4. Define one or two pivotal differences that separate them.

5. Brainstorm several win-win solutions. Come up with at least three, since, in the real world, the first answer doesn't always work.

Win-Win Worksheet

What are the situations and interests of the two parties (goals, needs, purposes, approaches, data, positions on issues)?	
What do the two parties have in common?	
On what do the two parties differ?	
What potential options might satisfy both parties?	

PART

IV

Accelerating
Teamwork

INCREASING YOUR TEAM'S PACE

With any luck, your team is approaching the norming stage after just a few days or weeks. Indicators of a norming team include:

- Enough stability to progress and get itself out of pitfalls
- Understanding team boundaries and emerging behavioral norms
- Shifting attention from blaming each other to solving problems
- Confidence to act like a team instead of individuals
- More consensus on issues and easier resolution of differences
- Moderate and increasing amounts of work accomplished

Here are some guidelines for improving mid-project teamwork.

- Adjust roles, goals, ground rules and processes
- Reaffirm procedures by working through rough spots
- Encourage improvements by recognizing progress
- Stretch the team
- Let them find answers to stresses on their own sooner rather than later
- Delegate functions as soon as the team can handle them

Team Action Plans

Teamwork requires the coordinated effort of multiple minds, mouths and hands. To accomplish this, the fastest teams plan their work and then work their plan. They focus on making progress one step at a time together, and they need the type of short-term tactics that an action plan defines.

An action plan is a series of specific tasks that a team works out in advance to reach a milestone. In their simplest form, action plans dictate who will do what, when. In their most detailed form, they contain:

- activities
- delegated responsibilities
- PR, training and recognition plans
- personnel

- solutions to human factors
- resources
- control systems

INCREASING YOUR TEAM'S PACE
(continued)

Team Delegation

Your team should build action plans to share responsibility, distribute workload and use everyone's talents, but some teams try to do everything together. Not only does this create unnecessary work, it's frustrating. Note how ABC's Distribution Team delegated tasks to individuals and subgroups.

CASE STUDY: ABC Distribution Team Action Plan

Here's the action plan ABC's Distribution Team developed for their booth at the next Computer Electronics Show.

#	What	Who (Reps from . . .)	When
1.	Design booth	Manufacturing, marketing, sales	June 5
2.	Purchase supplies and equipment	Sales, finance	June 10
3.	Build demos and visuals	Computer	June 12
4.	Arrange booth and materials shipment	Marketing	June 12
5.	Design employee training session and prepare handouts	Sales, quality control, finance	June 12
6.	Plan employee booth assignments	Team sponsor	June 13
7.	Conduct employee training session	Team leader	June 15
8.	Supervise booth assembly	Manufacturing, quality control	June 20
9.	Supervise booth operations	Team leader	June 20–22
10.	Supervise booth disassembly	Manufacturing	June 22

CONSENSUS DEFINED

The speed of team progress depends on how quickly and effectively members pool information and backgrounds and agree on goals, plans and actions. This effort can be subverted when everyone has a different view, strong-willed people won't give in, some dominate conversation, easy-going members avoid conflict, members won't express an opinion or some change the subject. Often the majority or the most powerful person decides.

Can RTD work this way and reach high performance? No, not if open participation is limited, minority views are rejected or team member input is ignored. Does this mean that every team discussion must result in an identical, unanimous view? Let's hope not.

The solution is to make key team decisions by consensus, which means by *general agreement*. Consensus is not usually one person's idea, nor is it everyone's first choice. Consensus is a decision reflecting the collective thinking of a team that all team members participate in developing, understand, believe is workable and will support. A consensus position is one that merges everyone's views.

How To Reach Consensus

To reach consensus, every team member must participate fully, be open-minded, offer solutions to differences and seek agreement. Cutting off discussion by asking for a majority vote will work against this process. Disagreements must be confronted and explored until win-win solutions are found.

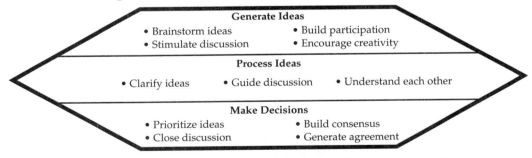

This approach to making team decisions is open and fair, but it requires more time and skilled facilitation to complete group discussion. Don't expect rapid consensus on every issue. Early in a team's growth, choose where universal support is vital, and use a quicker decision scheme for less vital situations. For example, consider using consensus to establish the team's charter, ground rules and project plans. Team conflicts should usually be resolved by consensus. Consider using a faster decision-making method such as majority voting or team leader choice for issues that may be noncritical, including meeting location, action item assignment and exact wording of minutes.

EFFECTIVE MEETINGS

Follow the rule: Plan your meeting and meet according to plan. If you don't get organized for an hour's personal work and operate only at 25%, you've wasted 45 minutes. If the same disorganization happens with a team of eight, you've wasted six hours.

An effective team meeting includes:

- clear goals
- published agenda
- prepared members and speakers
- full but focused participation
- time control
- public recording of ideas
- group process management
- closure

High-performance teams demonstrate equal input, balanced participation and shared leadership. They raise thorny issues, debate them heatedly and digest consensus out of confusion—and they do it in unison, getting the best out of each other without wasting time or ignoring input.

Meeting Hats

How do they do it? Practice helps, but they also have figured out a scheme to share meeting control and decision making. Although there's no mandatory arrangement, here's one way to rotate tasks.

- ► **Meeting chair.** Organizes the agenda, calls the meeting to order, announces items, assigns roles, asks for closure (usually the team leader)

- ► **Discussion moderator.** Asks questions, balances participation, regulates dominators, keeps the group on track

- ► **Timekeeper.** Notes timeframes, watches the clock, announces time remaining and deadlines

- ► **Recorder.** Itemizes points on flipcharts and takes notes

The division of labor works well this way, but do whatever works for your group. Just make sure each shares the burden.

PROJECT MANAGEMENT

Many team sponsors think empowerment means to leave the team alone; however, abdicating total control ultimately backfires. Healthy teams grow a sense of responsibility to the organization, respond to being held accountable and feed on a challenge. So a key rule of accelerating progress is to stay in touch.

Managing a team project occurs in five distinct stages.

1. START-UP

Insure plans are documented and reduced to small, measurable chunks, insuring that first steps succeed

2. MONITORING PROGRESS

Keep the team on track by establishing and monitoring checkpoints, requiring action plans for new milestones and adjusting master plans as needed

3. REINFORCEMENT

Recognize even the smallest wins; remind the team of commitments and provide needed coaching, training and rewards

4. TROUBLESHOOTING

Investigate troubles quickly, run interference with outsiders, conduct problem-solving meetings, encourage the team to take swift correction or propose changes with complete staff work

5. WRAP-UP

Recognize finished steps, complete loose ends, document progress and lessons learned, publicize results and celebrate success

MONITORING

A team should keep track of what it does and how it succeeds so it can reinforce what works or correct what doesn't before it's too late. A good monitoring system should be:

- Quick and easy to operate

- Reliable and accurate

- Frequent enough to show positive and negative trends

- Based on team goals and objectives

- Reviewed soon enough to take action

What should a team monitor to improve its operations? What should a team sponsor monitor to insure team accountability? Remember the basic rule of monitoring—that which gets measured, gets done.

Any team with a decent charter and master plan will have defined goals, key deliverables and SMART objectives based on customer requirements. You know that you want to measure satisfaction, quality or productivity—but that's not easy, especially when teams try to measure themselves at weekly meetings.

Many people struggle with establishing performance measures to quantify team progress, which are hardest to define when you insist on scientific precision. That's really unnecessary in a continuous improvement scheme like team building. You don't need a perfect scoring system to indicate performance trend. Here are some measures you can use to track three aspects of teamwork.

Task Progress

- Percentage of roadmap steps completed

- Number of weeks ahead or behind master schedule

- Percentage of action items completed before each meeting

- Percentage of improvements implemented

Meeting Effectiveness

- Number of team members attending each meeting

- Percentage of meeting time spent on team tasks rather than details or conflicts

- Range of team member participation during meetings

Team Maturity

- Percentage of initial training completed

- Stage of team development (forming, storming, norming)

- Score on Team Performance Rating Form (13 points on page 5).

You can probably define more specific measures tied to the team's charter. Until a team is self-sufficient, self-regulating and self-correcting, let the team facilitator judge softer dynamics such as empowerment, process awareness, commitment and consensus.

CASE STUDY: ABC Performance

ABC's Distribution Team measured initial progress using the following benchmarks, which were graphed, reported and reviewed weekly.

- Number of team members attending each meeting

- Percentage of action items completed before each meeting

- Number of weeks ahead or behind master schedule.

Once product shipments began, they also monitored:

- Number of units shipped by product

- Value of units shipped by product

MONITORING (continued)

Action Register

It's easy for a team to lose track of its activities in the midst of a busy work schedule. Many teams use their minutes to document any action items established in meetings. Action items record the assignment of *who* is responsible for doing *what* by *when*. Put these on the front page of the minutes so they don't get ignored.

Some assignments take longer than the time between team meetings. If you don't review action items, they're easily forgotten. An action register is an RTD tool that can help prevent loose ends. Here's a form for an action register and what you would list in each column.

Priority Level	Action Item	Assigned To	Date Due	Date Complete

Team Self-Monitoring

When a team's future rests in the hands of others who read reports months later, little improvement occurs. That's why the best monitoring is real-time self-monitoring. To do this, high-performance teams establish checkpoints, solicit feedback and analyze their performance. Then the team can reinforce, adjust and react to what's happening sooner.

Consider the following ways a team can monitor itself. Which would you like your Case Study Team to employ?

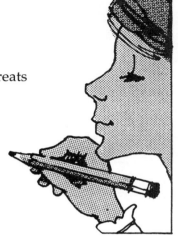

✔ Meeting Reviews By Open Discussion

✔ Group Process Checks By Team Members

✔ Team Process Observations By Team Facilitator

✔ Team Training Sessions and Team-Building Retreats

✔ Team Troubleshooting Meetings

✔ Individual Coaching Sessions

✔ Peer Performance Feedback

✔ Project Checkpoint Presentations

Coaching

Leadership has its place, but if you use too much command and control with a team, you can stifle motivation, energy and commitment. On the other hand, you can't ignore a situation that could be improved. Coaching is the solution.

A coach is a mentor who advises another, provides direction, gives feedback, reinforces what works and suggests ways to improve. This is how all team players should interact with each other. The team sponsor coaches the team and team leader about the project. The team facilitator coaches them and the team sponsor on group dynamics. The team leader coaches team members on their assignments and they coach each other and outside co-workers. When there's an opportunity to do things better and quicker, coaching works.

EXERCISE: Accelerating Teamwork

List at least three acceleration tools to put to work with your Case Study Team.

1. _____

2. _____

3. _____

UNSTICKING STUCK TEAMS

If your team-building has succeeded, your team has arrived at high performance. If you're not so lucky, your team may be stuck. Many teams run into a major obstacle, get distracted or never seem to get organized.

Unsticking ABC's Stuck Team

After several weeks of progress with one distribution channel, ABC's Distribution Team lost some focus and found their meetings going round and round no matter what they did. Here are some approaches to unstick them, arranged in order of how dramatic each solution would be.

Revisit Basics

Situation: The team has lost sight of why it was formed, or the situation has changed requiring refocusing or even disbanding the team

Solution: In a retreat or series of long meetings, have the team reconsider its purpose, review how its strategies are working or adjust its long-range goals by reworking the team charter

Update Master Plan

Situation: The master plan was never completed, the situation has changed or the team has strayed from its path

Solution: Have the team scan the situation, validate what works, rethink its approach, consider alternate strategies, update milestones and then rework its master plan

Think Smaller

Situation: The team is floundering because of a challenge that's too great for the time and resources allocated or its members' skill levels and stage of development

Solution: Scale back the charter's scope and size of its milestones, have the team seek smaller wins and increase the challenge as confidence grows

Inject New Information

Situation: The team's foundations are solid, but it seems to be aiming in the wrong direction, focusing on unimportant details or operating under delusions or false assumptions

Solution: Refocus the importance of the challenge, feeding them new information or having members get out and talk directly with their customers and suppliers about their circumstances

Training

Situation: The team lacks technical or group dynamics knowledge, skill or experience, and the gap blocks progress

Solution: Survey the team's strengths and weaknesses, design a retreat to achieve a quantum jump and follow up with just-in-time training

Team-Building Retreat

Situation: The team hasn't progressed through its storming stage fast enough to handle the pressure of its performance challenge or strong members; maybe some changes have caused a relapse

Solution: Interview team members to let them vent and identify issues, handle individual conflicts elsewhere, then convene a retreat to open lines of communication and solve common problems using the Troubleshooting Tool (see page 115).

Adjust Team Membership

Situation: The team lacks critical skills or experience and isn't developing quickly enough; some members aren't contributing

Solution: When individual attitude adjustment through coaching doesn't work, change some members' status to consultant and add replacements who have missing skills or attitudes

UNSTICKING STUCK TEAMS (continued)

Adjust Leadership

Situation: The existing team sponsor, team leader or team facilitator isn't guiding and developing the team fast enough to meet its obligations

Solution: Negotiate a face-saving status change, promote and train an existing player to the new role or (in the worst case) bring in an outside consultant to recharge the team

Rewards

Situation: The team is progressing, but they don't feel that their contributions are valued enough or they're losing heart by hearing too much criticism

Solution: Rebalance overall feedback to 80% positive versus 20% advice, increase individual recognition, introduce a small-wins-based team reward system and hold more celebrations

These suggestions don't do you much good unless you apply the right solution to the right situation. Use the Troubleshooting Tool to find your way to unsticking a stuck team. The four main headings represent the key logical stages for internal problem solving. The questions within each heading suggest alternative ways to help a team diagnose a resource gap, resolve a conflict or get the team back on track.

Troubleshooting Tool

Problem Description

1. What do you know about the problem?

2. Who is involved and how are they affected?

3. What obstacles impede what goals?

4. How do things differ from the way we want them to be?

Cause Analysis

1. What forces contribute to the problem?

2. Why does the problem exist?

3. What started the chain of events that brought us here?

4. What is the root cause?

Solution Decision

1. What strategies would resolve the situation?

2. How can we be sure to resolve the root cause?

3. How do the possible solutions compare to each other?

4. Which is the most workable solution to achieve our goals best?

Implementation Plans

1. What actions are required to solve the problem?

2. Who needs to do what to implement the decision?

3. How long will each step take?

4. What resources are needed to implement the solution?

UNSTICKING STUCK TEAMS (continued)

CASE STUDY: ABC's Solution

Here's how ABC's Distribution Team worked out of their doldrums using the Troubleshooting Tool.

Problem Description	Lost focus in meetings. Some team members lost their motivation. Aggressive schedule requires increasing pace, but loss of energy is slowing the team down.
Cause Analysis	More sensitive team members were unsure if what they're doing is right because of limited recent feedback. Team sponsor, Chris, has been in Europe most of the previous two months setting up a Continental sales force.
Solution Decision	The team's proposal to promote Lynn, the original team leader, to the sponsor role was accepted by CEO Terry. Now Lynn reports directly to Terry, assuring quick action if needed.
Implementation Plans	Lynn immediately authorized two delayed distributor contracts. Lynn arranged a feedback session with Terry to review what's working, what's not and plan for improvements. Terry bought the team an expensive dinner complete with French wine sent by Chris to the team. Terry reviewed where ABC would have been without the fantastic contributions of the Distribution Team. As a result, morale soared.

EXERCISE: *Troubleshooting*

1. Recall some team problems you've experienced or heard about.

2. Select one problem situation that could affect your Case Study Team.

3. If the situation should stall your Case Study Team, plan what you would do using the Troubleshooting Tool Worksheet.

Troubleshooting Tool Worksheet

Problem Description	
Cause Analysis	
Solution Decision	
Implementation Plans	

ADJUSTING TEAM MEMBERSHIP

Sometimes, despite your best efforts, the problem lies not in the process but a person—one specific team member. In that case, start at #1 and proceed only if needed.

1. Team members give private feedback to their teammates and the team leader about the problem.

2. The team leader coaches the team member based on existing contracts, team ground rules and common perceptions, asking for team facilitator help if necessary.

3. The team leader asks an outside authority such as the team sponsor or the team member's immediate supervisor to clear up any misunderstandings or conflicts on issues like time, goals or priorities.

4. The team leader conducts a group problem-solving session on the team's situation without blaming the team member.

5. The team sponsor changes the team member's status to that of consultant who doesn't attend all meetings or participate in team decisions.

6. The team member willingly agrees to leave the team.

7. Team sponsor replaces the team member.

Incorporating New Team Members

Whether it's necessary to fix a problem or just because people move on, team membership won't remain stable forever, and when the players change, team dynamics also change. You've got new personalities to adjust to and new skills to exploit.

Since high-performance teamwork grows out of the agreements forged by a developing group, even the most valuable newcomer creates a new set of problems. Should you start team-building all over? It's unlikely that you'll have the time and support for that. Should you just hope the newcomer gets accepted eventually? That's risky for the individual and likely to slow down teamwork.

Here's a program the team leader can follow to incorporate new team members into the mainstream.

Contracting	Meet with the newcomer to define expectations for participation.
Welcome	Publicly welcome and introduce the newcomer to the team.
Personal Contacts	Have each team member talk with the newcomer individually so they all get to know each other.
Mentor	Appoint one team member to acquaint the newcomer with team procedures.
Documents	Give the newcomer a copy of all team documents, including team charter, ground rules, plans, data, minutes and reports.
Brief	Brief the newcomer on team history, ground rules, procedures, processes, charter and plans.
Role	Give the newcomer a defined role to enable participation from the beginning.
Involve	Insure the discussion moderator encourages equal newcomer participation in team discussions and assignment of action items.
Coach	Give the newcomer feedback to reinforce what's working and advise how to improve participation.
Audit	When the newcomer is ready, ask for a personal audit of team structure and performance, scheduling a formal report including recommendations on the team agenda.

PART

V

Team Wrap-Up

WRAP-UP

You've worked hard to build a unit that has worked harder and smarter than a group of individuals could have separately. Now their charter is complete. It's time to move on, but your team doesn't want to break up. What can you do? You have three options.

Extend the team's charter	So they can have more responsibility for implementation, greater scope in their assignment or additional milestones.
Recharter the same group	To tackle a new challenge with a new project.
Disband the team	Redeploy the team members in jobs where they can use their talents or as the nucleus of new projects.

We've already covered the tools for the first two options. The third is the trickiest, especially if you hope to recruit motivated people to deploy future teams. Here's where the fifth stage of team development comes into play: adjourning.

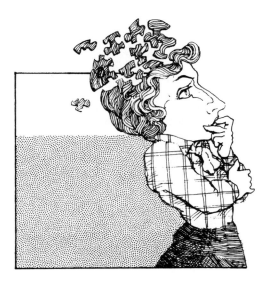

THE ADJOURNING STAGE

Many managers and teams don't devote the attention necessary to complete the job. There are new fires to fight and new ambitions to satisfy, so they abandon the old project and rush off to the new challenge. Still, human beings crave and benefit from closure. To achieve it, wrap up your project effectively with these four key actions.

#1: Final Report

Don't reinvent the wheel. You need to document what your successful team did so others can benefit from your experience. Insure the team develops a comprehensive project description, including:

- a brief summary

- the process or problem studied

- key data collected

- pivotal decisions made

- mistakes, obstacles and solutions

- technical and process lessons learned and their impact

- accomplishments

- implementation methods and status at the time of completion

This document will serve as your organization's primary written reference for the project. If your team has maintained a notebook of plans, data and minutes, the final report shouldn't be an impossible chore. Enter the report into a team and process history database. Whether or not the project was worthwhile, the final report will be.

#2: Final Presentation

Although your team has undoubtedly been meeting and debriefing the team sponsor right up to the end, plan a final summary presentation to close out the project. Invite senior management, stakeholders and even external customers. Prepare snazzy color visuals and refreshments. Of course, you'll want to hand out copies of your final report.

#3: Recognition

Recognizing team member contributions is not just a nicety that management should feel obligated to do, it's the key to making RTD work in the future. Rewarded behavior is repeated, but word gets around when management secretly believes teamwork is an effective tool to exploit workers and get something for nothing. Money is a nice reward for good teamwork, but is not the point. Giving credit where credit is due is crucial to the team process.

Further, high-performance team members undergo tremendous personal development. Because of their joint efforts, the members of a successful team are now experts in the problem or process they studied. This work should be reflected in performance reviews and promotions, but these people are also invaluable as future team builders. Using successful team members as ambassadors not only gets the word out, it's great recognition.

Finally, because of all the trauma, stretching and long hours, management really does owe the group one last company-funded party. You know that high-performance teams have more fun and celebrate more often than regular people, so make your final bash worthy of their accomplishment.

THE ADJOURNING STAGE (continued)

#4: Deploying Results

The previous three actions help deploy the lessons learned to maximum advantage. However, sometimes a task force's recommendations are ignored by those with the power to improve things. Don't let your team's project results die this slow death. Instead, apply some or all of these suggestions.

- Don't let the team disband until implementation is complete or at least well underway with their guidance

- Insure they develop and install a continuing control system to prevent past problems from recurring

- Distribute their final report or have it published as a technical article

- Have them make their presentation at other facilities

- Put key team members to work on developing training materials so their newfound expertise is never lost

- Have them train anyone who could benefit from what they learned

- Reassign team members as the nucleus of new teams who can profit from their experience

- Promote team members to new jobs where they capitalize on their personal development, technical knowledge and team expertise

ABC WRAP-UP AHEAD . . .

CASE STUDY: ABC Wrap-Up

After nine months, ABC's distribution scheme, though not yet making anybody rich, was starting to operate smoothly and seemed able to handle dramatically increasing volume. Some team members had such a positive experience that as the planned wrap-up date approached, they began lobbying to extend the team charter. With some difficult public soul searching, the team, with Terry, Chris and Lynn in attendance, decided that the Distribution Team had achieved its goal and should disband.

The team planned to assemble their records into a final report. The Distribution Team presented its summary for each department, top management and the board of directors. Unexpected by the team, Terry arranged for public recognition in front of board members for contributions above and beyond the call of duty. Commendations were presented and copied to personnel files.

Terry, Chris and Lynn met with each member and discussed how best to deploy Distribution Team expertise throughout ABC. Terry asked several members to lead new project teams, Chris delegated responsibilities to insure that team lessons wouldn't be forgotten and one earned a long vacation with management's blessing. One even volunteered for a challenging new assignment no one had been willing to tackle. When the team facilitator, Pat, checked with team members weeks later, they all felt, although they missed the Distribution Team, they were motivated to do more of the same elsewhere.

THE ADJOURNING STAGE (continued)

Personal Summary

Before you go off to use RTD's tools, look back at the first chapter.

1. Review the priorities you set on the book's objectives on page x. Which of these did you achieve?

    _____

    _____

    _____

2. What were the main benefits you found valuable from RTD?

    _____

    _____

    _____

3. What pitfalls do you especially want to avoid when deploying teams?

    _____

    _____

    _____

4. What are your plans for using RTD?

    _____

    _____

    _____

NOTES

NOTES

NOTES

NOTES

OVER 150 BOOKS AND 35 VIDEOS AVAILABLE IN THE 50-MINUTE SERIES

We hope you enjoyed this book. If so, we have good news for you. This title is part of the best-selling *50-MINUTE™ Series* of books. All *Series* books are similar in size and identical in price. Many are supported with training videos.

To order *50-MINUTE* Books and Videos or request a free catalog, contact your local distributor or Crisp Publications, Inc., 1200 Hamilton Court, Menlo Park, CA 94025. Our toll-free number is (800) 442-7477.

50-Minute Series Books and Videos Subject Areas . . .

Management
Training
Human Resources
Customer Service and Sales Training
Communications
Small Business and Financial Planning
Creativity
Personal Development
Wellness
Adult Literacy and Learning
Career, Retirement and Life Planning

Other titles available from Crisp Publications in these categories

Crisp Computer Series
The Crisp Small Business & Entrepreneurship Series
Quick Read Series
Management
Personal Development
Retirement Planning